THE DEVIL
INSIDE

How my minister father molested kids
in our home and church for decades
and how I finally stopped him

JIMMY HINTON

Endorsements

The Devil Inside is, hands down, the absolute must-read for every seminarian, seminary instructor, and church leader and volunteer out there. Without mincing words or sanitizing descriptions, Jimmy Hinton contextualizes the predatory sexual abuser in the very place he/she belongs: right next to you and me. Using real-world comparisons and analogies, Hinton addresses head-on theological problems of redemption and forgiveness and care for others exactly as Jesus would have him do. He cares deeply for the abused and wounded, makes space for the truly repentant, and offers a chilling description of the wolf in sheep's clothing.

Christine Fox Paker, MA, MACM
President/Executive Director, PorchSwing Ministries, Inc.

In his book, The Devil Inside, Jimmy pulls no punches. He lays bare his soul and puts in black & white precisely why we should and how we can better defend children from sexual predators.

His unapologetic approach and practice, when it comes to the protection of children and exposing sexual predators, should be an example for us all. If we all truly followed Jimmy's lead, we could virtually eradicate child sexual abuse.

As he says, "Resisting (evil) means we must take a stand for the innocent and vulnerable. It means we must choose righteousness and justice over comfort, no matter what."

Dave Pittman
Executive Director, Together We Heal
Child Safeguarding Trainer, GRACE

I recommend this compelling story of a minister's family forced to make a painful choice - protect their father or protect children from their father? From within their Christian belief system, they struggle with issues of faith, family, and forgiveness--includes educational discussions of psychology and patterns of behavior among sexual predators.

Abbie Fitzgerald Schaub, storyteller in "The Keepers" documentary

As a child protection advocate, The Devil Inside is a sobering reminder of why we advocate on behalf of victims. Pastor Hinton's personal experience reminds us that we cannot "monsterize" child sexual offenders because they blend into the community as ordinary members of society, making them easy to miss. The Devil Inside also serves as a wake-up call for the church and seminaries – understanding abuse, how it happens, and prevention must be an integral thread in the church's fabric. Finally, Pastor Hinton introduces the reader to a deeper understanding of Jesus and how He intentionally taught His disciples. This book is a must for every pastor, ministry leader, and seminary student.

Joe Harvey-Hall, KeepSAfe Director, The Salvation Army

Jimmy writes about what he knows. And what he writes, you need to know for it may save those you love. Had I had this information years ago, my own family might have been spared the horror that destroyed us. This is a book that needs to be read by church leaders and church members alike!

Les Ferguson Jr., Minister and author of Still Wrestling: Faith Renewed Through Brokenness

Published by Freiling Publishing, a division of Freiling Agency, LLC.

P.O. Box 1264,
Warrenton, VA 20188

www.FreilingPublishing.com

ISBN 978-1-950948-61-1

Printed in the United States of America

Table of Contents

Foreword

Plenty of religious leaders talk the talk of preventing sexual abuse in churches. Too often, their fine-sounding talk leaves a trail of destruction because it is nothing *but* talk. Pious preaching and empty platitudes don't protect kids.

When abuse hits close to home, in a pastor's own church or on his own turf, that hollow, unholy reality comes to roost. It's why clergy sex abuse runs rampant in Christendom. Many experts name churches as among the most dangerous places for children.

But Jimmy's story is an exception. His is not a story of talking the talk but of walking the walk. After sitting in his church office listening to a person tell of having been sexually abused in childhood, Jimmy walked into a Pennsylvania police station and turned in his own father, a beloved longtime pastor who had been a role model for Jimmy himself becoming a pastor.

This kind of courage is rare. By and large, pastors and churches deal dreadfully with reports of clergy sex abuse, too often choosing to turn a blind eye, to engage in minimizing self-deceptions, or to advance tactics for institutional protection. I know this because I've spent 17 years engaged with advocacy and justice issues for survivors of Baptist clergy sex abuse. Almost every survivor I've ever listened to – and there have been hundreds – has said that the trauma from how religious leaders responded far exceeded the trauma from the original sexual abuse. This was my personal experience as well.

Imagine if you can. As horrific as childhood sexual abuse is, those who experience it say that even *greater* damage is done by the institutional betrayal of the faith community, as so many respond with complicity instead of care, and silence instead of justice.

But Jimmy chose to respond with action. In the weeks that followed, as the list of victims grew, Jimmy learned more and more about the horrors of his dad's crimes. Jimmy's action surely spared countless other kids from life-altering harm, and it manifested true caring for those already wounded. In the words of Rachael Denhollander, the former gymnast who helped bring serial sex offender Larry Nassar to justice: "The extent to which one is willing to speak out against their own community is the bright line test for how much they care."

Jimmy passed that bright line test with flying colors. But lest you imagine that, once the abuse was reported to police, this story wrapped up easily or had a tidy "happy ending," Jimmy also recounts in significant detail, and without self-pity, the costs that came with what he did. The truth may set you free, as many will say, but the truth can also exact a toll. It's a toll that most are unwilling to pay, preferring the status quo over the seismically altered terrain wrought by the truth of clergy sex abuse.

Having navigated this terrain himself, Jimmy now offers some important lessons. They are lessons not only for the Church but for all who care about the safety and well-being of children.

As Jimmy explains, pastors who prey on kids employ specific tactics of deception, and they are quite cunning in what they do. When we minimize their abusive conduct as though it were some hapless "mistake" or as merely "falling into sin," we deny the predator's intentionality and we do so at the peril of children.

With insights gleaned from conversations with his dad in prison, Jimmy digs deep into the "how" questions. *How* do sexual predators get away with abusing kids for years while no one suspects? *How* do they so wholly deceive us? *How* do they lead a double life? *How* do they target their victims? And more hopefully, *how* can we proactively intervene to disrupt the patterns of deception *before* they result in abuse?

Thank you, Jimmy, for your hard-hitting honesty. I pray there will be many who take your lessons to heart. And then, "may justice flow down like waters" from an undammed river of truth.

With hope for a future in which children are safer,

Christa Brown
Author, This Little Light: *Beyond a Baptist Preacher Predator and His Gang*

Prologue

I cleared the lump from my throat and reached for my wife's hand. God knows I needed her comfort. "There's no easy way to tell you this," I said with hesitation. We were both sitting in the living room of some dear friends. I explained to my friends, "My dad sexually abused your daughters." I could see the devastation on their faces, and they could feel the pain, sorrow, and embarrassment in my heart. I sobbed uncontrollably as my wife held my hand. "I'm sorry. I'm so, so sorry," I kept saying. They were the only words that came to my mind, and I know they did little to provide comfort or answers for the parents of these little children who were abused by my father.

Abuse is evil, cruel, and incredibly common, especially in the church. Every researcher and advocate acknowledges that abuse is rampant in religious communities, and it's not getting any better. I live in Pennsylvania, home of Jerry Sandusky, Bill Cosby, and the infamous 2018 Pennsylvania Grand Jury investigation into the Catholic church. The prevalence of abuse in the church reminds me of a small town in Pennsylvania called Centralia. Centralia used to be a quiet coal mining town of 1,500 residents, but on May 27, 1962, the town was forever changed. Five local firemen intentionally set fire to a landfill that was near a coal strip mine. The landfill had been decommissioned, and the town was forced to move it. Town council minutes do not specify how the cleanup of the condemned landfill was supposed to happen, and some speculate that the burning procedure was never recorded because burning landfills was against the law. The landfill fire was extinguished the same night by the same firemen who started it, but a couple days later, flames erupted again. The firemen learned that the fire had found its way through a hole that led to an underground coal mine.

In an alleged effort to cover their own tracks, city council members did not reveal how the fire started when they asked miners' unions to inspect the fire. Several proposals were put on the table immediately, but local laws and other red tape kept anyone from taking any immediate action to extinguish the flames. Several exploratory holes eventually were drilled, but those only added oxygen to the shafts, fueling a small fire and turning it into a raging inferno. To this day, the fire burns on and is unstoppable. Tens of millions of dollars have been spent on fighting a fire that could have easily been extinguished at first. All but five residents of Centralia were forced to leave. Most of the buildings in the town have been razed, leaving little evidence that a town ever existed. Some estimate that the underground fire will burn for another 250 years. What was once Centralia, Pennsylvania, is now a wasteland and a spectacle for curious onlookers and thrill-seekers to come and watch it burn.[1]

Like Centralia, the church has done little to address abuse early on. It is now an unstoppable force because, time and time again, people chose, and still choose, to turn a blind eye. A 2008 study by the Centers for Disease Control found that the total "estimated financial costs associated with just one year of confirmed cases of child maltreatment (physical abuse, sexual abuse, psychological abuse and neglect) are approximately $124 billion."[2] This study was done long before the rise of human sex trafficking. The fire is spreading, and is only getting bigger.

James 4:7 says, "Resist the devil and he will flee from you." I believe in resisting evil. But believing in resisting and actually resisting are two very different things. To do so, we need to know how the devil operates. Otherwise, we will never see the one who is actively ravaging souls, even when he stands right in front of us. *The Devil Inside* is not a book about a cover-up. It's quite the opposite. This book tells the story of just how calculated and deceptive abusers are, and how evil was inside my house and church for decades without any of us knowing it. Like the hidden hole that swallowed the landfill fire, evil will always thrive in environments where we refuse or don't know how to uncover the devil's schemes.

I will share my journey from the perspective of a child growing up with a loving father. Then, once the abuse was revealed, I share why I reported my father to the police. Finally, I offer a strong theology of a protective God who calls us to action. While the spread of abuse is unstoppable in my lifetime, I believe the church has a strong obligation to resist the devil and start making the church safe again. We can slow the spread of abuse, but the more we wait, the harder it will be. This book is a story about a small-town Pennsylvanian who defied the odds and fought the devil face to face. Churches can do this. They *need* to do this. Our churches need to simultaneously provide healing for survivors of abuse and become safe shelters for the innocent and vulnerable. With God's help, we can protect many lives and start extinguishing the hidden flames that are raging beneath the surface.

Chapter 1

MY CHILDHOOD HERO

The show *Genius Junior* blows my mind (no pun intended). The show is made up of literal geniuses who are all around ten years old. The mind truly is a gift from God, and it's miraculous to see what it is capable of. In the last episode I watched, contestants were asked if they remember what their first memory was. None of them could pinpoint their very first memory, but they all said age two was as far back as they can recall some of their memories. The earliest memory in my mind is still as clear as if I were actually there. I was three or four years old, and I remember riding shotgun on the way to preschool. I still remember the new car smell of the little Toyota. This was the early 1980s, long before strict car-seat laws, so sitting up front was common for us kids. My treat was getting to shift gears for Dad on the five-speed manual as we made the eleven-mile trip down country roads to my daycare. He was so patient teaching me the shifting pattern and made me feel as if shifting gears was the most important job in the universe.

Learning to shift gears would have its payoff. At the age of ten, I remember walking outside to find two shiny red Honda 125cc three-wheelers! One was for my older brother Tim, and the other was mine. I couldn't believe it! They each had a four-speed manual transmission with a semi-auto clutch, which meant there was no manual clutch to pull for shifting gears. We rode hundreds of miles on those little things and formed thousands of incredible memories. My left shoulder still bears some pretty cool scars from a minor accident that left me scraped up and bleeding (thanks, Tim). Dad was always generous and loved to do big surprises for us kids.

One day my siblings and I walked outside to find a brand-new brown Oldsmobile station wagon sitting in the driveway. We inspected every inch of that beast, and I still remember wondering why the gas pedal was so huge in that thing! Dad popped the cassette tape in, cranked up the volume, and the Oldsmobile jingle started playing: "There is a special feel in an Oldsmobile!" That cheesy song is etched in my brain forever. We must have played it a thousand times. We had no shame belting the jingle out to people walking down the sidewalks as we drove by. Dad was always the cool dad who let us goof off and didn't care what other people thought. We were a tight-knit family having fun, and nobody could rob our joy! We were always encouraged to be ourselves. We kids felt so cool in the "way back," as we called it. The third row seat faced the rear door that had a roll-down window. It was always a treat when Dad would roll the window down and let us hang our heads out as he drove up our long gravel driveway. The dumb window always got stuck as he rolled it up, but he would put it down for us anyway.

Then there was the 1978 four-speed manual Ford F-150 that he bought just as a junker to play with around our property. Mom hated that truck. The exhaust ended right behind the manifold, and that thing was deafening! Every time the driver let off the throttle, it would send a series of backfires and huge flames out the tailpipe. It sounded like a 12-gauge shotgun being fired in rapid succession. We lived on 23 acres of secluded land, and the keys were always in the ignition. Any one of us kids could drive it whenever we pleased. I was the only one who drove it constantly. I couldn't wait to get home from school so I could fire up the beast and rip around in it. The whole town knew when we were home from school because they could hear that junker crack like thunder. When I pushed the heavy clutch, my small nine-year-old frame didn't allow me to see over the steering wheel. No matter—once it was rolling, I would prop myself up with my elbow against the seat, push the gas with my big toe, and spin the tires on our gravel driveway. It was all fun and games until one day I saw blue flashing lights behind me.

I would routinely take it to the bottom of the long driveway and, because I wasn't tall enough to see to back it all the way up the driveway, it seemed safer to turn around on the road. At least that's how my nine-year-old brain reasoned. Our driveway merged onto a state highway that happened to be on a blind corner where cars whizzed by at 45 mph. I had just turned around at my usual spot and started back up the driveway, spinning tires as I always had. I saw the flashing lights, pushed in the clutch, and stopped. "Yes, officer? Was I speeding?" Looking back years later, I don't know how the man kept from laughing!

"Sir, the reason I pulled you over is because you turned around on a public road. May I see your license and proof of insurance?"

I'm pretty sure he was just toying with me at this point. I could play his game, too, I thought. With a straight face and my heart beating out of my chest, I calmly replied, "Sir, I must have left my wallet in my bedroom."

It worked! The state trooper let me go with a stern warning not to do it again. The trooper followed me up the driveway and tattled to my mom. I was sure I'd be grounded for life, but all she did was yell at me and threaten to take away the keys if I did it again. The road is impossible to see from the house. She had no idea I was turning around on the dangerous corner. For all she knew, I could be driving miles up the road—not that I would have ever done that!

One time I stole my oldest sister's friend's station wagon and took it for a joy ride around our property. I'll never forget his face. One minute he was standing on the porch talking with my sister and her friends. A moment later, he watched me casually climb into the driver's seat of his old Dodge station wagon. I honestly think he just assumed I was an innocent kid playing in his car. I mean, what nine-year-old preacher's kid steals cars anyway? I am reason number one why we should never assume! The keys were in the cupholder. Keys to me were more tempting than candy. Candy tasted good for a few seconds, but car keys had the potential to provide hours of fun!

I tried to put the key into the ignition of his car, but no matter what I did, it wouldn't fit. I realized that the key had to go in upside down (maybe this is why I never liked Dodge cars!). Bingo! As soon as the key fit in the ignition, the car was started and the tires were spinning on the gravel. I had lots of experience driving, and knew how to drift rear-wheel-drive cars sideways around corners. *Dukes of Hazzard* was my favorite show, and it taught me a lot about how to properly handle a car! I was a tiny little stunt driver, for sure. A few years ago, I saw Steve, who owned the car, and he said, "Do you remember the time you stole my car when you were a little kid? I still can't believe you did that!"

"I was just teaching you to always keep your keys on you, and that you never know who you can trust, Steve." I smiled just a little, looked him in the eye, and said, "You're welcome."

The swimming pool was another favorite surprise for my siblings and me. One day a group of workers showed up and were smoothing a sand pile. We had no idea what they were up to. We guessed that we were getting either a beach or a sandy playground. With Dad, surprises were always grandiose. Then within a couple of hours, a brand new 24-foot-diameter pool was upright and fire trucks were lined up, filling it with water. The following year, we had a large deck built around the pool. We spent endless hours in that pool over the years. My brother Tim and I would get back from a long three-wheeler ride, jump into the pool to cool off, and then hit the trails again. Life was the way it was meant to be for a kid—carefree and happy. We had it all: ATVs, a pickup truck, a swimming pool, bicycles, and 23 acres of bliss where we could run wild and nobody bothered us.

Our ten-mile trip to church was usually pretty eventful. There were already nine kids in the family. I am the sixth kid, so we had to get creative in how to arrange our seating in the car. We'd all cram into the station wagon. I would be in the way back, sandwiched between my two older brothers. We would fight like cats and dogs. Yelling, punching, name calling, and tattling were what made the ride fun for us kids and miserable for our parents. Mom would yell back at us, which only intensified our fighting. We thought it was funny to get her worked up. Dad was always the calm one. He would occasionally threaten to spank us with his belt if we didn't behave. Every now and again, he would make good on his promise. We knew when it was coming because there would be an eerie silence just before we pulled up the driveway. He would open the back door of the station wagon and, one by one, give us a single crack with the belt. Honestly, it didn't hurt much at all. But, boy, did it hurt our pride. We still went back to fighting every single trip we made in that mobile wrestling ring. I have fond memories of fighting with my brothers.

The fighting eventually got so out of control that Mom bought us all boxing gloves. I think it was her way of giving up on trying to keep us from fighting. At least this way there would be padding when we punched each other. We turned it into a fun boxing game! We spent hours and hours boxing each other. Even as young kids, we knew to set rules so that nobody could take a cheap shot and hospitalize the opponent. Dad was always laid back and calm and didn't mind us fighting as long as it didn't get out of control.

It didn't take long for boredom to set in, and we figured out how to make "welt masters" by wadding up my brother Chris's baseball cards. We'd roll them as tightly as we could, pull back on the thick rubber bands, and let them fly. Getting hit by a welt master was worse than any punch. A direct hit would create an instant welt on the skin, and screams of pain always ensued. Unlike boxing or wrestling, this felt like a real battle because it left very definite battle marks on the skin. The shooter was proud that he injured his opponent, and the wounded felt proud to show off the battle wounds. There were holes all over the drop ceiling in our bedroom from misfires. Hearing those shards of cardboard coming at us was terrifying. A miss was a good thing, but that sound of it hitting the wall would make us jump a mile high.

Christmas was always our favorite time of year. We kids were allowed to stay up as late as we wanted and watch our favorite holiday classics. Presents were always put under the tree on Christmas Eve. We believed in Santa, and one year I actually saw a glimpse of him putting presents under the tree! The bedroom I shared with my two older brothers was in the basement, and we were forbidden to come upstairs. Our parents must have known that we would go up because "Santa" was putting the presents around the tree. To this day, I still don't know if Saint Nick was Dad or if he had someone else dress up and come over. I only ever remember having one Santa sighting, but I look back and find it odd that there was actually someone dressed as Santa putting presents under the tree. Dad and Mom always went all out for Christmas. There is not a single bad memory of that holiday. It was always a magical time of the year, and our parents worked hard to give us an incredible Christmas.

Vacations were the same. Because our family is so large, we would do two separate vacations. Beach trips with my brothers were so much fun. We'd go to Ocean City, Maryland, every year. Dad would always roll the windows down when we got close so we would hear the seagulls and smell the ocean water. As I type this, memories are flooding back into my mind and I'm smiling. Those vacations helped shape who I am today, and I want to give my children the same experience I had growing up. We were given freedom to roam, freedom to laugh, and freedom to behave like children.

I had a godfather named Jim when I was growing up. He happened to be my dad's boss from his job selling life insurance. Every year, he would take my dad and me to Annapolis on a sailboat trip for several days with his employees. I was the only kid on the boat, and none of my siblings got to go on this annual vacation. I felt very spoiled and a little bit guilty about that. We'd sleep on the boat while docked at a small island. I saw my first Lamborghini on one of those islands. I was into cars from a young age, and Lamborghinis were my absolute favorite! I felt like the coolest kid, and for good reason. Everything about those trips was incredible—the anticipation of going, the excitement of traveling, the smell of the ocean, getting to pilot the boat, dipping my toes in the water as we sailed her across the ocean, and exploring the small islands where we would dock. Jim was genuinely a kind man, and I cherished getting to spend my time with Dad on those trips.

Those bonding times are part of what shaped me into the man and father I am today. My father always treated me with kindness and taught me to respect both women and adults. The values that were instilled in me as a kid made me the person I am today because of the love I was shown by my father. Having the freedom to be independent, learning how to fight and resolve conflict, and being able to live a carefree life were gifts that every child deserves. I feel so blessed in so many ways as I look back at the childhood I was given. So many kids grow up with parents who fight, get divorced, or who beat and humiliate them. But my childhood consisted of love, respect, and lots of laughter.

My siblings and I were never allowed to disrespect adults. I remember when I was seven years old and telling my mom to shut up. I don't even remember what she said, but I half-jokingly told her, "Shut up!"

As quickly as I said it, I felt my dad's hand come across my face. He had a way of disciplining where the shame felt much worse than any physical pain. The slap wasn't hard, but it got my attention. He looked me in the eye and said, "Never, EVER talk to your mother that way. Do you understand?" I got the message and have never spoken disrespectfully to her since that day.

My dad was my childhood hero. I never wanted to disappoint him. He provided everything for our family, and he often talked to me about the importance of treating everyone with fairness and compassion.

Chapter 2

A CALLING TO MINISTRY

Do you ever just know what you were meant to do for the rest of your life? It's kind of like when you find the right mate. I never dated anyone until I met my wife. When I asked my mother how I would know who the "right one" was, she gave the unhelpful answer, "You'll just know." Thanks, Mom! But you know what? She was right. When I met Natalie, I knew immediately in my gut she was the one I'd marry.

My middle son is seven years old. He knows he's going to be a paleontologist. He digs in our yard for hours looking for dinosaur bones! He has mountains of books on dinosaurs and can properly identify and pronounce every dinosaur currently known to man.

Some kids just know what they want to be when they grow up. Those dreams can change, of course, but it's the certainty and confidence that kids have that I'm talking about. I knew at a young age that I wanted to preach, and it all started with my admiration of my father.

I logged hundreds of hours sitting at the feet of my dad as he preached. He was a good preacher. He had a way of using metaphors, and he was a good storyteller. I remember getting lost in his stories. They were often funny. Sometimes they were sad. Other times they were gripping and full of suspense. He always knew how to read his audience and would respond accordingly. I can still hear his favorite mantra replaying in my head: *"This is where the rubber meets the road."* Application was very important for him. Even as a kid, I remember wanting to apply what I'd learned on Sundays as soon as church dismissed.

Sundays were a time to get lost in thought. I studied my dad's every move. I clung to every word. When I got a little older, Dad would let me help him make copies of his sermons that had been recorded on cassette tapes. He had a machine in his basement office of our home that would make one copy at a time. It recorded them at lightning speed—about five minutes per tape! I remember thinking that one day I would get to have my sermons on cassette tapes. I beamed with pride for my preacher father, and wanted to be just like him, minus the suit! I've always dressed casually, and suits don't match my personality one little bit.

He always wore a suit with a tie and heavy jacket. It didn't matter how hot it was—he always wore his suit jacket. I only wear a suit when I preach a wedding or funeral. If my congregation didn't mind, I'd wear shorts, sandals, and a semi-dressy T-shirt. But not my dad. He was always dressed to the nines. He looked professional. He sounded professional. And his preaching made me want to join the ranks.

Dad never tried to convince me to become a preacher. In fact, when I expressed interest, he almost tried to talk me out of it. My mom worked very hard to talk me out of it. In fact, she *begged* me not to go into ministry. Looking back, I understand why. Ministry is hard. It's especially hard on a family. It's hardest on the minister's wife. Ministry is full of joy, disappointment, failures, births, weddings, baptisms, funerals, and a host of people who pledge allegiance to God and the church but who eventually leave for one reason or another. People come and go all the time. Every time a family leaves, it feels like a divorce for the minister and his family, and it always makes me question what I might have done to cause them to leave.

It's a curious thing. People will leave a church or not ever go in the first place, but they still look to the minister for answers to life's biggest problems. Whether it's a marital crisis, an addiction they are battling, attempted suicides, a family death, or advice on which car to purchase, the minister is usually the first person people call on for help. This is an honor for the honest minister, but it's an *opportunity* for someone who is an abuser. I'm now eleven years into full-time ministry, and I've logged nearly one thousand hours in teaching and preaching alone. That doesn't count the endless hours of visitations, premarital counseling, dozens of weddings, lots of funerals, and many phone calls I receive each week when people are in crisis.

Ministry is about helping people and expecting nothing in return. Sadly, though, in smaller churches, the majority of people you sacrificially help end up leaving the church anyway. The amount of criticism and conflict within the church is often depressing. There is good reason why the burnout rate is sky-high among church leaders. The point of this isn't to make anyone feel sorry for me or for me to paint a negative picture of the church. My point is that, as a kid, I had no idea what was hidden behind the façade of Sunday morning smiles and artificial greetings. I had no idea because my dad never complained. Ever. He always seemed to enjoy preaching. He didn't ever seem flustered or frustrated.

So, as a child, my calling into ministry was only sharpened and romanticized. By the time I was eleven years old, I was working full time on a farm just up the road from our house. I loved it because I got to run heavy equipment. At age eleven, I was driving tractors and pickup trucks—a skill I had learned when I was younger. I remember telling my farmer friend who hired me at that age that he made a good choice because I already had lots of experience driving!

Dave, the farmer I worked for as a kid, is an incredible man I'm deeply indebted to. He is a hard-working Christian man who instilled in me both a strong work ethic and a sense of honor and respect. He taught me the value of patience and determination. He spoke freely about God but never shoved it in my face. To this day, I have the utmost respect for him. Failure was never an option on the farm, and no matter how bad things were, my boss never complained. Unlike church culture, my boss didn't pretend there weren't any problems on the farm. Instead, we acknowledged problems, worked on them as a team, and got back to work as quickly as possible. There was almost a magical rhythm to troubleshooting and fixing issues that came up.

My whole life, I was surrounded by godly men who were patient and kind. I sat in the church pew daydreaming about speaking to crowds of thousands of people. As Dad preached to the small church of 65 people, my mind would wander to a day when I would be speaking to thousands. This dream was not about having a big platform, but it was about helping lots of people transform their lives. It was about speaking hope into the hearts of people who were desperate to find Jesus who would love them back. A boy can dream, right? I had an idealistic picture of peace and happiness, because that's all I ever knew.

My calling only grew stronger when our youth group would take weekend trips to youth rallies. The Churches of Christ have regional youth rallies where hundreds and sometimes thousands of teenagers gather. Organizers bring in top-notch speakers, and there was always something magical about traveling to go to these big events. Many of my best childhood memories come from going to the rallies. My dad took us to every youth rally, and we would always sing our hearts out in the back of the station wagon. We usually had several vehicles that would caravan. My dad drove the lead vehicle, which I always wanted to ride in. Everyone fought to ride in my dad's car. He would goof off and let us all sing, tell jokes, and do whatever we wanted. When we neared our destination, excitement would build. We'd pull up to a stoplight and Dad would yell, "Chinese fire drill!" It was a form of musical chairs, but with cars. We would all pour out of the doors, circle each of our cars, and dive into the nearest door before the light turned green. Sometimes we would wind up jumping into one of the other cars, if it happened to be the nearest to us at the time.

Those rallies created a lot of incredible emotions. Everyone was happy—ecstatic, really. The music was moving. The speakers were out of this world! I remember hearing Jeff Walling, who was one of the best-known speakers for youth rallies at the time—and for good reason. Jeff was (and still is) down to earth. He was relatable. He was funny. And Jeff is a gifted storyteller. Jeff could turn a dictionary into a portal leading to Narnia. His talks were moving and motivating, and they always led to genuine transformation.

Jeff would be a guest speaker years later when I was at college. One of my best childhood friends followed me to college and was sitting beside me. He'd battled drug addiction throughout high school. Jeff was only ten minutes into his talk, and my friend's shirt was soaked from tears. Jeff was specifically talking about overcoming substance addictions and how we are created to be worthy—worthy of love, honor, and self-worth. Jeff is authentic. People believe the message because they believe Jeff. I still love to hear him speak at our lectureships. My good friend later confessed his struggles with battling addiction and was baptized.

As a child who already felt a strong calling into preaching ministry, I became more sure when I would hear Jeff speak at rallies. His audience was large, and the same kids who were goofing off moments before were mesmerized and clung to his every word. Listening to Jeff became my first real introduction to the gift and art of preaching. I wanted to learn Jeff's art—not because I wanted to be good at preaching, but because I have always been a believer in helping people's lives to be transformed, and the spoken word happens to be the best way for that to happen.

Farming gave me ample opportunity to daydream. Many of my younger days were spent strapped to a tractor seat. Nine solid hours of driving provide abundant time to allow a kid's mind to wander. I would imagine my audience. I could see their faces. My sermons would slowly take shape, and I would work them and rework them in my mind. Trees on the edges of the fields would turn into people's faces. In my mind, I could see the pain in people's eyes and feel their desperation to be given hope. Sometimes I would be moved to tears, and that's when I knew I'd homed in on something important that had depth and had the potential to connect.

I wasn't preaching as a kid, but the hours of daydreaming combined with pew time listening to my dad preach every Sunday all reinforced my desire to one day grow up to be a preacher. That would change for a season when I got to college, but eventually I came back to my childhood calling. After attempting a business management major for a semester, I abruptly changed my major to earn a B.A. in Bible and religion. As much as I hated my business classes, I loved my Bible classes even more! This confirmed that I had made the right decision to follow my dream of going into ministry.

Later confirmation would come in the form of a recruiter for seminary. I'd never even considered getting a master's degree. School was always more of a time to socialize and goof off, and college was no different. My college years were spent procrastinating with my course work and finding new places to camp, hike, and explore with friends. I was not an honor student because I had no desire to apply myself to anything other than having a good time with friends! So it really surprised me when I was being pursued for a four-year master's program. The master of divinity degree is rigorous and is eighty-four credit hours. Most master's degrees are thirty-six credit hours.

After visiting the campus of the seminary, I decided that the program wasn't for me. But the recruiter kept telling me that he saw something special in me. I assured him that I was a mediocre student at best, that I had no desire to apply myself to school work, and that I wasn't positive I even wanted to preach. He said none of that mattered. He was insistent that I at least consider it, and I was insistent that I didn't want to pursue a master's degree.

I'm the type of person who doesn't like to be pressured. If I feel even the slightest bit of pressure to make a decision, I will either dig my heels in or do the exact opposite. Much to everyone's surprise, upon graduating with a degree in Bible, I started calling different trucking companies to inquire about becoming an over-the-road truck driver. Growing up on the farm gave me a taste for running heavy equipment, and I always loved to travel. It seemed a natural fit, then, to get paid to travel for a year. I was still single, was only twenty-one years old, and was ready to hit the road.

In August of 2001 I got my commercial driver's license through Schneider National's truck driving school. I had three weeks of training followed by one week of driving over the road with a trainer. After four weeks, I was sent to Connecticut to pick up my very own truck and first load. I was officially all on my own.

That first load was going from Connecticut to Dallas, Texas. I had several extra days to get the load there, so I decided to stop in at my parents' house for a couple days. I parked my rig at the farm in Shanksville where I worked as a kid. I got some much-needed family time and then climbed into my truck and continued on. Two days later, I was entering the Dallas city limits when I heard some truckers talking over the CB radio about an airplane that had just crashed into the World Trade Center in New York. I was stunned when, minutes later, they were talking about a second plane that hit the other Twin Tower. I turned the radio on, and every station was broadcasting live. I was pulling into my destination as the third plane crashed into the Pentagon. "We are officially under terrorist attack," the broadcaster said. "This cannot be coincidence."

I backed into the dock and, after getting unloaded, continued to listen to the live broadcast as they said that a fourth plane went down somewhere in a field near Shanksville, Pennsylvania. My heart sank. I was literally there just two days prior. My parents have the largest field in the town of Shanksville. It took several hours to get through to any family members, but I was relieved to find out that United 93 landed in an old strip mine I used to frequent, just one mile from my parents' house. Everyone in the small town of 230 people was spared.

Seeing the reign of terror on innocent people that day affected me greatly. I was always taught by my parents to love our neighbors and do no harm. My heart was shattered for the three thousand people who lost their lives on 9/11 due to the cruel, selfish acts of a handful of terrorists. It didn't take long to decide that I now *needed* to go to seminary. All the hours that I spent daydreaming about preaching had to be for a reason. I was resisting ministry, and ministry kept pulling me back in.

I was committed to one year of driving with my company, but I wanted the seminary recruiter to know that I was ready to commit the next four years to getting my master's degree. It was more important than ever that I followed through. I needed to put my money where my mouth was and actually apply myself to studying the Bible and learning how to be better equipped for serving and teaching people. I would finish my year of driving. After exactly one year, and over 100,000 miles later, I quit the company and began seminary, fulfilling my childhood dream of going into the ministry.

Chapter 3

PENNSYLVANIA BOUND!

Because a bunch of my friends were still in college, I decided to move back to Arkansas where they were and make the two-hour commute to Memphis, twice a week, to seminary. For the next four years I would remain in Arkansas, where I also met my wife. We both worked as graduate assistants, and we instantly felt a connection. My mom was right. When we find true love, we "just know." Natalie and I began to date in the spring of 2004, and in July of 2005 we were happy newlyweds!

We continued to live in Arkansas until I was done with my coursework. It wasn't our favorite place to live, but we managed. My wife and I do not like the heat. Okay, that's an understatement. We *loathe* the heat. As much as I hate the heat, I love the cold even more. I began extreme cold exposure training a few years ago. Really—it's a thing. It's called the Wim Hof method, and it's a combination of a breathing technique followed by gradual exposure to the cold. In a very short time, I can train my body to be exposed to extreme cold for long periods. I've trod many barefoot hikes in the snow, completed several ice water swims (breaking the ice with a sledgehammer is tougher than the actual swim!), and gone for hours of snowshoeing in nothing but sandals, shorts, and a T-shirt. Last year I completed a 9-hour hike in 25-degree weather wearing nothing but shorts and sandals. It requires a little bit of training and a lot of dedication, but I love doing it, and the health benefits are incredible.

I lived in Arkansas for a total of nine years, beginning in 1997. One day in January of 2007, we decided we had enough of the southern weather. We packed up a moving truck and drove to Pennsylvania as a "temporary" stopping place until we found out where we wanted to take up residence.

The heat drove us north, but the bigger reason we moved to Pennsylvania was because my mom and dad had recently separated. Because I had been living 1,000 miles away and was focused on graduate school, details were not really clear surrounding their separation. It wasn't something they advertised to the world. All I knew was that, after 30-some years of marriage, they just couldn't get along anymore. News of their separation left all of my siblings and me in a complete state of shock. The entire community was shocked along with us. Mom and Dad were held in very high regard by everyone. We were the model Christian family, and they were the model parents. Then, after raising eleven children, they suddenly pulled the plug on their marriage.

Every time I spoke with Dad on the phone, he sounded sad. He never seemed resentful toward Mom, but he expressed how hurt he was that she wanted to leave him. The more I spoke with him, the more I felt sorry for him. From his perspective, Mom was completely shut off to him and wasn't treating him with kindness, and he didn't know why. I rarely spoke with Mom about their relationship, but for several years my siblings and I could see how increasingly frustrated she was with him. She would often argue with him and say that he intentionally said and did things just to irritate her. Around 2000, he left the Somerset Church of Christ and started his own house church. It was at the house church that I witnessed how combative my mom had gotten toward Dad. In hindsight, I found out that my mom was simply worn out from the years of lying and deception that we kids didn't see. Like all of us, Mom never suspected my dad of sexual abuse. However, there was another controversy that rocked our family. In the mid 1990s, Dad knowingly worked for a fake company that bilked elderly people out of over $5 million. One of the people he ripped off was an elderly church member. He took $30,000 of her retirement money. In July of 2002, my dad was sentenced to one day in federal prison and was ordered to pay $1.16 million in restitution. I was there for his sentencing, and I remember how well my dad made it sound as if he were a victim.

Pittsburgh's *Trib Live* says:

> The former insurance salesman and pastor of Stony Creek Church of Christ allowed unethical people to use his good name and relationships to rob his former clients, the prosecution charged. ... He testified during the trial that there was a moment six years ago when he realized the insurance scheme was dirty, and his wife advised him to turn back, but he pressed on. Hinton broke down on the stand remembering that moment. Hinton told U.S. District Judge Donald J. Lee that he felt shame over the deception that was deeply out of character.
>
> "To this day, I do not understand why I was vulnerable to give in to this thing," said Hinton.[3]

My dad was under investigation by the FBI for several years, and our house was full of constant tension. Mom believed in his innocence and worked around the clock to research attorneys and gather information for them. I remember her being upset that, during the investigation, my dad still wanted to go back and work for the fraud who hired him. Nothing seemed to bother my dad about the scheme, and that always got under Mom's skin. She couldn't understand why her health was declining from stress, but my dad was acting as if nothing had happened.

By 2007, my parents were separated, my dad was broke and had nowhere to live, and Natalie and I were looking to start our careers. Just prior to moving to Pennsylvania, I asked Natalie if we could take my dad in when we moved. She agreed that we could take him in temporarily until he got on his feet again. After all, in our minds, he was sad, had been kicked out of his own home, and had gone through a series of job changes that left him with little income. We felt guilty not giving him a place to live, so we caved.

We learned fairly quickly that our "temporary" stop in Pennsylvania was becoming more permanent. I drove a semi-truck again for one year to make money while we figured out what we wanted to do. It wasn't ideal to be trucking after graduating from seminary, but it paid the bills. Year one turned into year two. The trucking company I drove for went out of business, and a good friend of mine gave me a job at his company selling commercial truck parts until I was offered a position as the preaching minister at my home church.

In June of 2009, exactly two and a half years after Natalie and I moved to Pennsylvania, I had taken a position as a full-time preaching minister at my childhood church, where I'm still preaching to this day. My wife got a full-time teaching job as a reading specialist the same month, and a few months later, we were handed the keys to our first home that we'd just bought. We had officially laid our roots down in the place that was supposed to be just a rest stop along the way to our unknown destination.

Prior to buying our home, my dad had lived with us in the rental house for almost two years. My wife began feeling the tension of having him live with us. He mostly stayed in his bedroom and would come out to eat dinner with us. He lost his job as a commercial truck salesman the first year of living with us, and in the second, he began talking about how neat it would be to be a "manny" (a male nanny). He was already a grandpa, he argued, and said that he loved kids, so he'd prefer to get paid watching them. We all thought that it was strange that a man who once boasted the title for best insurance salesman in the state of Pennsylvania was now flat broke, still owed $1.16 million restitution, had nothing in retirement, and was happily living with his middle child and wife while pursuing a "career" as a manny making $10 per hour.

Several of my siblings thought it was strange that he wanted to be a part-time professional babysitter at the age of 59. Though we all thought it was uncanny, I don't remember any of us using the word "creepy." Odd, definitely. Financially foolish, absolutely. But, believe it or not, none of us expressed how creepy it was, probably because he never really gave a creepy vibe. Even though it was bizarre, he had a way of making it sound really normal and fitting to his personality. But he increasingly became obsessed about this job. We talked to him about getting a job at Lowe's or Walmart. If he was so broke, why was he pursuing a manny job the next county over for less money and fewer hours, while driving 100 miles a day when gas was hovering at $4 per gallon? He would have been hired immediately at Walmart. It made no sense why he pursued the manny position, but none of us thought much more about it.

Natalie and I bought our house in September of 2009. By this time, tension between her and my dad was running thick. He had been living with us for two years and had no intention of getting a job that actually paid anything. Though we didn't charge rent, he never offered to pay us a dime, either. He bragged about being on food stamps. When we started looking at houses, he talked about how nice it would be to live with us in a bigger house. He never asked whether it was okay to move in with us in our new house. He framed it in a way where it was assumed that he was coming along. He said, "I may live with you and Natalie a couple more years. Then I might find another family member to mooch off of in another state. It's nice to get to travel for free, and I would love to visit different grandkids."

His casual, matter-of-fact statement to "mooch off" another sibling did not sit well with me. I told Natalie what he said, and it ignited a flame inside of her. Her reply was, "We're buying this house, and your dad doesn't come with it. Find a way to tell him, or I will." I still felt sorry for him, but there was no convincing Natalie to let him live with us. And I was okay with that. She was right. He was an adult, and it was time he began to act like one. He needed to get a decent job and take responsibility, the very thing he taught his kids to do.

I got the preaching job three months before we bought our house. A good friend of mine who I met at seminary was preaching at Somerset and decided to go back and work on a doctorate in Texas. Because I was already living in Somerset and attending the church, because they knew me for many years, and because my dad had preached there for almost three decades, I was first on their short list of people they were considering.

We weren't even looking for a house, either. We casually looked at some online just to see what the housing market looked like in our town. We saw an old farmhouse that looked neat and went to see it with absolutely no intentions of buying it. It was love at first sight. We are *not* impulse buyers by any stretch of the imagination. Ever. But this house truly felt like home for both of us. I was hired at the church in June of 2009. We closed on our house in September, and in May of 2010, our first baby girl arrived! Within eleven months, we had new jobs, a new home, and a newborn baby. It was a lot of good changes that came in rapid succession, and we felt incredibly blessed by all of it.

Things were going exceptionally well at the church. I had just turned 29 when I was hired. They had me write out my vision for the church as part of the hiring process. I'm a visionary thinker, so it was actually a lot of fun for me. The church, like many small churches, had a long history of problems. My farming days of addressing problems and solving them came back to me. I'm a believer that existing problems need to be addressed and that change is possible as long as people are willing to put hard work into correcting bad attitudes and behaviors.

There was an excitement that was building within the church, and the sleepy church I once knew had movement. We were planning mission trips together. Our vacation Bible schools were a blast and were drawing in larger crowds than we had seen in a long time. Unchurched people were visiting, being baptized, and staying. We really witnessed things steadily moving in a very good direction, and there was no doubt in my mind that God was behind it all.

To understand my enthusiasm for our growth, it's important to understand how unlikely the change was that we experienced. I don't think I can overstate how difficult the small church culture is in the Northeast. Churches are closing their doors at an alarming rate, and the Northeast region is becoming more and more unchurched by the hour. The statistical likelihood of turning a small, 100-year-old church around is almost an impossibility. It just doesn't happen.

We had met all the criteria for a dying church. Thom Rainer, who has studied church trends and consulted with hundreds of churches, estimates that churches exhibiting the signs he outlines have greater than a 99 percent chance of closing their doors.[4] We had all the signs of a dying church, plus quite a few bonus ones. We were the poster church for a doomed congregation. But things were turning around. People were happy. They were excited to be there. They were loving their neighbors well. And we were steadily growing. I started to wonder if Jesus was wrong when he said a prophet is not welcome in his own town. This was the church I grew up in, and I was welcomed with open arms!

I was thankful for my training at both the university and seminary levels for ministry. The start of my preaching ministry brought me back to the year that I began driving a semi-truck. The first time I was in an 80,000-pound truck by myself was terrifying. Driving a big rig is a lot of responsibility, and I was responsible for a lot of lives. My training was crucial to my ability to navigate the seventy-foot-long semi-truck with skill and accuracy. Trainers set up orange cones, and we had to make tight turns with the behemoth of a truck. The goal was to hug each cone with the trailer tires without bumping or knocking it over.

It requires a great deal of confidence, focus, and finesse. But we were warned that overconfidence is a recipe for disaster. So is complacency—getting too comfortable with ourselves and letting our guard down, even if for a second, was the quickest way to get into a serious accident. We were shown gruesome pictures of crashes where truck drivers had glanced down at a map or were distracted by a phone. The trainers instilled the seriousness of always paying attention and having an awareness of the amount of responsibility we had as operators. We were warned that the driver, and the driver alone, is responsible for the space around the truck. "Don't let other drivers intimidate you into making mistakes—*you're* the one behind the wheel," my instructor warned.

I remember how terrified I was on my first solo trip. Four weeks of training—three in a classroom and one on the road with an instructor—and I was completely on my own. But after those four weeks, I was equipped enough to spread my wings and keep growing. Visions of mangled trucks kept flowing through my brain. The gruesome photos and stories the trainers shared were motivation enough to maintain focus and professionalism. I wanted to be like my one trainer who had over four million miles accident-free. He had all my respect, and it was his humility that caught my attention. The four-million-miler told us he rates his skill level at a 3 out of 10 because he has so much more to learn.

With preaching, I had not just four weeks, but almost nine years of training under my belt. Though I was (and still am) incredibly grateful for my training, I realized that training for ministers is very different from training for professional drivers. Ministry training is exceptionally heavy on lecture and very light on mentoring. Bible students are taught to think and speak, not to live with much of a sense of "street smarts." Conversations of deception and abuse in the church were completely absent from my training.

I felt very equipped to think, but not nearly as much to lead. To be honest, I can't recall any specific lesson on what biblical leadership really looks like. It's assumed that leaders make all the decisions, as if they hold all the answers without including the church members. Preachers are the educated ones, the trained professionals. In case you can't tell, I'm not a fan of leaders holding all the power. Jesus didn't shut "common people" out of the conversation. He invited them in. The reason my trucking instructor rated himself a 3 out of 10 is because he said we must always learn from other drivers, even the inexperienced ones. This trainer's lesson was not lost on me, and it certainly wasn't taught in seminary, either.

In seminary I was not taught to serve and disciple people as Jesus did. Think about my truck driving training for a moment. Four weeks! They showed gruesome pictures of accidents from negligent drivers and warned us not to lose focus. Jesus, when he trained his disciples, didn't put them in a classroom for nine years. He told them to follow him and painted a gruesome picture of what would happen: "Behold, I am sending you out as sheep in the midst of wolves, so be as wise as serpents and innocent as doves. Beware of men, for they will deliver you over to courts and flog you in their synagogues" (Matthew 10:16–17 ESV).

Jesus told them to be humble, removed their rose-colored lenses, warned them to watch out for deceptive people, and sent them out into the community—on their own! Contrast what Jesus said with what most of us are taught about treating everyone with respect, no matter what. Turn the other cheek. Don't cause ripples. Grow the church. People are safe once inside the church. Smile and nod along, and be the leader who has the answers.

I'm not trying to paint seminaries in a negative light. I got a top-notch education, and I still highly recommend my seminary to people. But I think most, if not all, seminaries in our country are failing to equip ministers to distinguish wolves from sheep. We are pretending that churches are safe when they are not. When abuse is disclosed, leaders have no clue what to do with the disclosure because it doesn't match what they were taught. I know, because a disclosure of abuse came to me, and I was caught completely off guard. Nobody—and I mean *nobody*—warned me that this was even a possibility in the church. Yet it is incredibly common.

I wish. I wish someone would have taught me how to be on guard for deceptive people. I wish I had been warned that abuse is common in the church. I wish I would have been taught about trauma. I wish someone would have told me that reporting abuse will change your life forever. But nobody did.

Chapter 4
WE NEED TO TALK

It was a sunny Friday in July of 2011, and my youngest sister, Alex, called me. "Can I come talk to you today?"

I could tell something was wrong. Her trembling voice gave it away. "Sure, what time?" I said.

That afternoon, Alex showed up and only said one word: "Hi." I invited her into my office at the church building, and she handed me a piece of paper and immediately sat down, crying. I began to read an email she had printed off between her and someone else in which they described an event years ago when they were both sexually abused by my dad.

Until that moment, I never had any reason to suspect that my dad had sexually abused anyone. The thought never crossed my mind. Where was this coming from? How long had he been abusing children? How many victims were out there? It didn't really matter at that moment, because answering those questions was not the reason my sister came to me. What mattered was that my baby sister was sitting in front of me, completely broken and expecting me to do *something*. I can't begin to imagine the courage it must have taken to walk into my office that day. It's been more than nine years and I *still* can't fathom her bravery. She will forever be my hero for mustering up the courage to tell me her painful secret that day.

Within a fraction of a second, it felt like a million memories flashed through my mind. And, to my surprise, they were weird memories. There was a time we were on a family hike at a waterfall just a couple of years prior. Two young teenage girls were in their swimsuits when they noticed Dad taking tons of pictures. Other times, he asked my wife and me if he could bathe our infant daughter. We always denied him, but I remember him offering several times. There were times he offered to babysit other people's kids so that he could "give them a break." There wasn't anything earth-shattering or anything at the time that we felt was completely out of the ordinary. But they were strange, unsettling moments. And there were enough of them in my memory bank that what my sister shared with me made absolute sense. I instantly felt the floodgates in my brain burst open while hundreds of these memories kept pouring out.

I knew she was expecting some kind of a reaction from me, so I looked at Alex and said, "I believe you." I composed myself and said, "I have no idea what's going to happen from this point forward." I was thinking that I could potentially lose my job, our family may need to relocate, and the whole world would know that my dad was a pedophile. I shared with Alex some of those thoughts but reassured her that none of those fears mattered. I continued, "What matters, Alex, is that *it stops now.*" Seeing my baby sister sobbing because of what our father had done to her made me rage inside. How could a father sexually molest his own daughter? Alex had been carrying this weight her entire life, and none of us noticed. I had a very strong feeling that if Dad could sexually abuse his own flesh and blood, there was no doubt that he was currently abusing children.

As soon as Alex left, I called my mom. I knew that she knew at least some of the details because she had given me a heads-up that Alex would be calling to meet with me. I told her what Alex had just revealed, and we both agreed that we needed to go into the police station together and report it. Believe it or not, I had no idea at the time that I was a mandated reporter. This was all pre-Jerry Sandusky. There was little public talk at the time about abuse. It was barely even on the radar. Nothing—and I mean absolutely *nothing*—was spoken about clergy being mandated reporters in seminary. Nothing was taught about screening or background checks. Not a word was taught about the prevalence of sexual abuse in the church or the need to have a written policy. I was completely flying in the dark, and I felt so lost.

Thirty minutes after Alex left my office, I was explaining to my wife what I had just found out. Thirty minutes after that conversation with Natalie, I was conducting a wedding rehearsal for church members who happened to be our very dear friends. I felt sick to the point of almost vomiting. People were smiling and laughing, and inside I felt as if my soul had been ripped out. The next day was their wedding. I don't remember much about that day. My mind was consumed with what I had just learned about my dad, and a wedding was the last thing on my mind. But I didn't have the heart to bail out of our friends' wedding the day of. Nor would it have been fair to share with the couple that I was dying inside. I could only pretend that all was well, hoping nobody would notice.

Not only did I have to push through officiating a wedding, but my dad happened to be a guest. He was all smiles, as usual. My dad had officiated the wedding of my best childhood friend—the brother of the bride—just a few years earlier. Dad had me read a scripture for that wedding. It wasn't uncommon for Dad and me to share responsibilities when either of us officiated a wedding. After the wedding in 2011, we went to the reception hall. We had assigned seats at the reception dinner. We sat at a round table—Natalie to my left, Alex to my right, and my dad sitting directly across from us. I could feel my heart in my throat. I worried about what Alex was thinking. I felt anxious knowing what I knew and having to sit across from *him*. Alex was abused by our dad and had to face him every single day of her life growing up. All I could think about was how I wasn't able to protect my little sister—not when she was young and was being sexually abused, and not at the wedding where her abuser was sitting just feet from her.

The thought of reporting my dad and the possible repercussions consumed me. Would he find out that Alex was the one who disclosed abuse? What would happen after we reported? Would he murder us in a fit of rage after getting caught? Would someone else kill him? Would he deny the abuse and be let off the hook? My mind was racing like crazy while my newlywed friends were dancing in the background. I couldn't remember a word I had said when I officiated their wedding. To this day, my only memories of their wedding are of sitting at that table. I can still see Dad's smile, completely oblivious that anyone besides his victims knew a thing about his secrets, and unaware that he was hours away from being reported for his crimes.

The next morning was a Sunday. I'm a laid-back speaker. A performer I am not. I'm usually put off by preachers who "catch the Holy Ghost" on Sunday morning and snap into character the moment they step on stage. With me, what you see is what you get. I am the same on Sunday that I am on Tuesday. But this Sunday was different. I got up to preach, and there he was. My dad sat in the second row, looking right at me. He always told me how proud he was of me. I wondered if he would be proud that I was just mere hours away from walking into the police station and changing his life forever. Like the wedding from the day before, my only memories I have of that Sunday are of his smiling face as I peered out at the congregation, my mind in a complete fog. Looking back, I have no idea how I even functioned. But I don't want this to be about me. Alex. Alex was sitting next to Dad. How in the world was she able to do it for all those years? It still blows my mind. Survivors are warriors. They must endure hell constantly. At this point, I was counting the hours until our small-town police station opened.

Chapter 5

TEARS AND FEARS

Finding out my dad was an abuser instantly brought me back to my childhood. I wondered why I was spared while my sister was abused. I would find out later that he abused other family members. I wondered how all of my memories with my dad were positive, while some of my siblings had completely different experiences. I wondered if I just was remembering wrong, or if he was just really good at living a double life. Nothing made sense at that point, and I couldn't piece anything together in a meaningful way. Finding out about the abuse created an instant identity crisis. I began to question *everything* about my life growing up as a kid.

I was an anxious kid. It's hard to put into words, but I was good at processing very heavy trauma, yet I was emotional when minor things happened. I remember when my friend Ritchie was killed. He was riding on his four-wheeler, something I had done every day since the day I got my new Honda three-wheeler. In rural Shanksville, kids rode their ATVs everywhere. We had ATV "gangs," sometimes with ten or more riders. We would just show up at friends' houses, park outside, and next thing you knew, we were off with one more rider. But Ritchie was riding alone that day when he crossed the road in front of a vehicle that struck him, and he died. My dad was the one who broke the news to me that Ritchie had died. Dad was so gentle in the way he broke the news. Ritchie and I had just hung out the night before, running down the halls at the school basketball game, goofing off, and laughing so hard our bellies hurt. It's strange, but when tragic events happened, Dad was always there to provide comfort. He had a way of making everything feel like it would be okay. He always spoke grace and kindness into tragic situations. Deep down inside somehow I always felt a great calmness wash over me after talking with Dad.

People tell me that I have a calming presence—that nothing seems to shake me, and that's what makes them feel safe around me. I hate that—not that I'm calming, but that I'm calming *like my father*. I often remind myself of him. And I hate that, too. When I know something horrible about someone, I tend to overcompensate and do everything I can to *not* be like that person. But what's the alternative to my father—to having a calming presence and an ability to express compassion? He often used it for evil, but even that messes with my mind. Were there times when he was genuinely caring? I have to think so, but I also know that prior to his arrest, he was using kindness as a technique to keep me unaware of his abuse. He would keep me incredibly close, but in a manipulative way. My wife recognized it before we ever knew he was a child abuser. So I struggle tremendously with the notion that I learned to be a calming person from *him*.

Being patient, calm, and kind is not a disposition. It's a *discipline*. Anyone who has ever worked with people knows this! Some people know how to intentionally push all of our buttons. Others are just naturally irritating. Some are obnoxious much of the time. Some are always negative, no matter how good they have it. I get annoyed with people. That's just a fact of life. But to remain nice and treat all people with kindness is a discipline. I have never snapped at anyone. It's not because I'm naturally calm. It's because I have to work very hard at being self-disciplined.

There was nothing that rattled my dad, and he had the same inviting presence that people say I have. I learned it from him. I can't overstate how much I observed every mannerism, analyzed every word, and felt every emotion from him when I was a kid. When I said he was my childhood hero, I was not just wasting ink talking about it. He really was my childhood hero. His ability to speak grace and wisdom into difficult situations is why we all trusted him. It was how God became real to us. It was how us kids learned to love and feel and live with joy.

There were so many times that we kids were unfair and downright nasty to each other. It's part of growing up and being a kid. Kids have no self-knowledge. When our kids are being ugly to each other and we address it, they have no clue what we're talking about. My five-year-old will punch or slap his brother and sister, and when we catch him, his favorite saying is, "Cameron made me do it." Correcting him and getting him to see that his actions are hurtful is a constant challenge. It's something that has to be taught. He will get it eventually, but with children, it takes years to develop self-knowledge.

My opinion is that many people are not taught, for whatever reason, to reflect on their inner self. Self-knowledge is an important life skill to develop, and it seems that masses of people don't possess it. I've known quite a few people who are mean or nasty or they have no filter when they talk. And they're totally clueless. I can talk with them about their poor behavior toward others and get blank stares back. Some people literally have no idea that they come off as being rude or selfish or demanding. That doesn't describe my family in the least. I'm proud to say that every one of my siblings has a tremendous amount of self-knowledge. We are all careful how we approach others. We know when we are crossing a line or being offensive to someone because we can see it on the other person's face. I honestly think that we learned much of this from Dad. He often would pull us aside and ask us if we were aware that our attitudes were hurtful to others. He really was good at getting us to think inwardly and reflect.

He never had to raise his voice. That was Mom's job! Really. We loved our mom and still do, but we were scared of her. I think most mothers can relate. Moms often feel like they're the bad one or the mean parent. Dad gets to come home from work, and the kids flock to him. "Daddy!" they exclaim. Mom isn't met with the same enthusiasm. Dad is viewed as the fun one. He is creative, fun, energetic, and cool. And Mom yells. This doesn't describe every home, but a lot of you mothers get it. This describes my childhood home to a T.

Dad is the one who bought us three-wheelers. Dad let us drive the old Ford truck. Dad bought our swimming pool. He played basketball with us in the driveway. He took us to ball games at school, spent countless hours with us outside, preached week after week, taught us the value of doing chores (man, did we hate those pesky chore lists!), spoke peace into our hearts when we were hurting, and taught us how to respect others. When I see kids who grow up without fathers or who live in homes where they're abused by either parent or by a parent's boyfriend or girlfriend, my heart shatters. Our home wasn't perfect at all, but it seemed to be full of love.

I use the word "seemed" now, because I'm not sure how much was genuine love and how much my dad was using us kids to practice and hone his art of deception. Our upbringing also was obviously very different for my sisters who were abused. I feel guilty that my memories of growing up are positive. At family gatherings, we don't talk about fun childhood memories for a few reasons. For one thing, it feels insensitive to my sisters if we boys talk about all the fun we had growing up. For another, all of our memories are twisted, confusing, and blurry. Nothing makes sense anymore.

We looked like the model American family. We were Christians. All of us kids were well-dressed, well-fed, and well-mannered, and we weren't viewed as some weird family. My older brothers, especially, were known as the "cool kids." They were good-looking and popular, and girls swooned over my two oldest brothers. My oldest brother, Mike, was a wild one growing up. He knew everyone in Somerset County and was the life of every party. Still to this day, I go places where people know my two oldest brothers. I was in New Mexico several years ago, and someone randomly approached me and said, "You're a Hinton, aren't you? I knew your older brothers Mike and Joe really well." I say all of this to give much-needed insight into abusers' homes. There is so much about abusers that researchers haven't explored, so people automatically make assumptions. We hear all the time about how manipulative and controlling abusers are. And they are, but it doesn't look like it or even feel like it to most people, *especially for kids.*

If we're looking for the Jim Jones cultish family where the kids are forbidden to leave the compound, we're looking in the wrong place with the vast majority of abusers. I've met many family members of pedophiles, and when I speak about our home life, it resonates with them. People often approach me in tears to thank me for understanding. The kids of abusers are normal people who are typically well-educated, well-spoken, easy to relate to, and super kind and compassionate. We generally can't look at children as a way to "find" pedophiles. Personally, I think that many people are so desperate to see signs in abusers that, more often than not, they create signs that were never there in the first place. I'm sorry to say this, but looking at the children is just not an accurate way to identify abusers unless those kids are severely abused and have clear, visible signs of distress. Knowing what I know now about abusers, if I were to go back in time and peer into my family as an outsider, I would never guess that my dad was an abuser based on the way we children behaved. There's got to be a better way.

Chapter 6

REPORTING

On Monday morning, Mom and I met at the church building and rode over to the police station together. I knew the detective, Ruthie Beckner, really well. I had worked as a truck driver with her cousin and officiated two of her nephews' weddings. We live in a small town, and everyone knows everyone. I knew Detective Beckner but didn't know how incredible she was as a sex crimes investigator. Mom and I had no game plan. How do you prepare for reporting the person who raised you? How on earth do you report your own father and best friend to the police?

As I mentioned before, even though I was a mandated reporter, this was not why I made the report. In fact, I had no idea at the time that I was a mandated reporter. Our state has raised awareness since the Jerry Sandusky and Penn State scandal, so there is no grey area anymore about who mandated reporters are. The real reason I reported my father was because it was the right thing to do. My mom and I never entertained any other options. We literally saw no other option before us. It wasn't a matter of *if* we would report him; it was a matter of *when*.

As silly as it sounds, Mom and I were using hypotheticals when we spoke with my detective friend. "What would happen if 'an adult' said that she had been sexually abused by 'another adult' when she was a small child?" We offered several different scenarios, all of them based on information we had. It must be the brain's way of processing the grief of it all. Hypotheticals allow us to still tell truths without naming the person. It's a form of keeping a safe distance emotionally.

Detective Beckner entertained several of our hypotheticals for a while. Then she smiled, leaned in, and firmly said, "All right. Cut the crap. You didn't drive down here to waste my time talking about hypotheticals. Who are we talking about?" I knew at that point there was no reason to keep my dad anonymous. Why were we trying so hard to protect *him*? We had nothing to hide. We did nothing wrong. *He's* the one who molested my little sister. Mom and I had vital information that could both spare many new victims from abuse and put an abuser behind bars for the rest of his life. Little did we know at that moment that that's exactly what would happen.

I can't speak for Mom, but I felt sick to my stomach. More questions were raised than we found answers for. As strange as it sounds, I still felt like I was betraying my father by reporting him. Looking back, I know how ridiculous this is. But it's how I felt at the time, and this is a big reason why people don't report abuse of close family members, colleagues, and friends. It's terrifying, and the brain works against itself when reporting someone you love and admire, because it makes no sense that the person we know so well could have such a dark side without us being aware of it. Outside the police station, life was going on as usual. My dad was still unaware that he was being reported by his own son and the mother of his eleven children. But inside the station, nerves were very thin. I felt like Judas, who gave Jesus a kiss on the cheek as he was betraying him. Just the day before, I still smiled, high-fived, and spoke with my dad as if nothing was any different. Now I was sitting inside a police station, committed to making a report that would forever change his life.

It all still seems so strange. Ironically, although I *felt* like Judas, my dad actually *was* Judas. He betrayed his victims in the worst possible way by publicly displaying harmless affection while secretly humiliating and sexualizing them. A few days went by after reporting. It seemed like an eternity. I was hardly functioning, and things were eerily calm. Then my phone rang. It came up as Somerset Police on my caller ID. My heart was pounding out of my chest. This could only mean one thing—Dad had been called in for questioning. A thousand scenarios ran through my mind. I picked up the phone, and detective Beckner said, "Jimmy, he just left the station, and it's bad. It's really bad. There are many victims, and this is one of the worst cases of abuse I've ever had. Be expecting a call from him. He still doesn't know you were the one who reported."

As soon as we hung up, my phone rang again. As she predicted, it was my dad. Panic doesn't even begin to describe what I felt. All the emotions that had washed over me a few days earlier were now a raging current, sweeping me away. I've never experienced a panic attack, but that phone call was the closest thing to having one that I can imagine. "Jimmy, we need to talk. Something very serious happened, and there are some things I need to get off my chest. Can you come over now?"

I told Natalie that I really needed to go meet with him. Though I couldn't put into words why I needed to, she understood. As I type this, memories of that night flood my mind. It was a hot, humid night. He was living in a small apartment by himself. Awkward silence filled the room. "What do you want to tell me?" I asked with genuine concern, afraid of what he would reveal that I hadn't heard yet.

Dad stared at the wall for what felt like an eternity. "I did some things that were blown out of proportion, and I may be spending the rest of my life in prison. I'm screwed. I'm really, really screwed."

For the next hour, I just let him talk. Any time I asked a question to clarify what he meant, he would evade the question and start making excuses. "We were just horsing around. You know how I always played with you kids. These little girls successfully depantsed me three times. We were just playing, I swear to God." Suddenly it felt like a complete stranger was standing in front of me. He had the face of my father, but his entire demeanor was different. This was not the father I knew growing up. My dad was a leader. He was always calm and collected, and he was the person I went to when I needed advice. Now I was asking basic questions about what happened, and he couldn't answer a single question with an ounce of clarity. The conversation was incoherent.

He didn't cry until I asked him if he was planning to kill himself. He never answered with words, but instead, he pulled three bullets out of his pocket and handed them to me. There was no gun in sight, so I didn't feel there was an immediate threat. I asked him very specific questions and determined that he did not, in fact, have a plan to kill himself. I can't ever know for sure, but the biggest part of me felt that the bullets were planned before I arrived to garner sympathy. I'm not a hunter or a gun expert. I own a couple guns that I just use for target practice. But I knew enough to recognize that none of the three bullets matched. One was a 30-06 bullet—from his favorite deer hunting rifle—and I can't remember what the other two were. But I remember it being very odd that he would mismatch bullets if he had, in fact, a plan to kill himself.

I tried to get him checked into the Behavioral Health Unit at the hospital, which was only a couple of blocks away. A 72-hour commitment would have done us all good. Instead, he insisted he was okay, and I reluctantly believed him. I've visited quite a few people in the BHU, and I know that unless there is an actual explicit threat to follow through with suicide, I was powerless to have him committed. Because he explicitly stated that he would *not* commit suicide, the hospital would turn him away even if I convinced him to go.

My conscience didn't allow me to leave him in the state of mind he was in, so I decided to stay the night. When I called Natalie to tell her, she was very upset with me. "He abused a bunch of kids, destroyed our lives, and now you're having a sleepover with him?" She hung up. The crazy thing is that I didn't disagree with her. She was exactly right. My mom needed me. Natalie and my baby daughter needed me. My sister needed me. And now my dad was the one getting my time and attention. And once again, he won. I felt like I was falling into an abyss of confusion and helplessness. I was damned if I did, and damned if I didn't.

The next day I went home and just sat in silence for a long time. I was trying to process it all: the odd behavior, the irrational talk, and the picture of Dad pulling bullets out of his pocket kept looping through my mind. The image of Alex sitting at my desk with her head in her arms vividly played on repeat in my mind. Officer Beckner and her notepad. The pain in Mom's eyes. The dancing bride and groom blurred in the background as my dad's smiling face came to focus in the foreground. The voices of my dad's victims who'd called me that week to tell me what he had done to them when they were kids. Words, images, and emotions were all flashing through my brain over and over and over again. The pain was pressing down on me, and the thoughts were way too many to process. Is this a small sample of what God feels every day?

I had been entrusted with so many secrets all at once. There were too many secrets—secrets that I didn't know how to process and that I wasn't prepared to process. Yet I had to keep a clear head because I had to make decisions, and I had to make them fast.

It was only a few days since Mom and I had made the report. Dad had confessed to the police, but he hadn't been arrested yet. Only a handful of my ten siblings knew. Natalie and I had chosen a very small group from the church who we initially told. I knew that I needed to tell the entire church soon, but we had so little information at this point that Officer Beckner said it might be best to time it for when he was going to be arrested, which would be any day. The main reason, and one I totally agreed with, was that we didn't want anyone from the church who was in denial to publicly defend my dad. The victims who were interviewed were extremely fragile, and it would have been detrimental if people began to rally around their abuser. It would not have been good if church members started defending my dad's "innocence" or spoke about all the good he had done his whole life.

I felt like I was lying, not telling the church. But I also knew how important it was to time it properly. I was assured that my dad would be arrested very soon and that, in the meantime, he was served papers that did not permit him to be near any minor children. That, combined with the fact that he was scared, brought me some sense of relief. He would have been very stupid to make any attempt to abuse a child after he had been served papers. He wouldn't risk it. I knew him, and he expressed to me how scared he was. For the first time in his life, his fear was something tangible that he couldn't hide. Fear of prison was controlling him, and it gripped him. For decades, this man reigned terror on little children. His victims feared my dad for all that he had done to destroy them. Now he was the one who was scared, not of what he had done, but of the consequences he now faced.

Chapter 7

TELLING MY SIBLINGS

The weekend after Alex disclosed the abuse, our church had a planned trip to one of our Christian universities in West Virginia for a Sunday school teachers' workshop. I was the one who organized the trip several weeks before. Just one week after Alex sat in my office, we loaded a van full of people from church to go down to Ohio Valley University in West Virginia. Excitement filled the inside of the van as people shared ideas for what would make our classrooms better for the kids. Kids—all I could think about were kids who had been molested by my dad. I wasn't in the mood for this trip, and I certainly wasn't in the mood to think about planning fun classes for the kids at church. As people laughed and shared ideas, my mind was a million miles away. I just stared out the window, steeped in sadness.

The university had just hired a brand-new president, Dr. Harold Shank, who happened to be my dad's old college roommate and best friend. As soon as we pulled into the parking lot, I spotted Harold and his wife Sally. They are two incredible people who both have my deepest respect. They have always been great friends of my family, and they still are to this day. Natalie and I were greeted with hugs from Harold and Sally. "How's your dad?" Harold asked. "I'm so excited to be so close to you guys now. Sally's speaking at your church event in

Somerset in a few weeks, and your dad and I are going to spend the day together catching up!"

I wanted to melt into the sidewalk. "He's doing great! He's excited to see you." I lied to one of the godliest men I know. And I had to. Half of my siblings didn't even know yet. I couldn't tell Harold before my family knew.

Not twenty minutes later, my phone rang. It was one of my brothers. "Is it true? What the hell is going on? Why the hell didn't you tell any of us?" I told him everything that I had found out over the past few days and explained why Mom and I hadn't contacted every family member yet. In the course of one week after my sister disclosed abuse, I officiated a wedding, preached a Sunday church service, reported my father to the police, found out there were many more victims, spent the night at my dad's apartment, took a van load of enthused church members to a college campus, and spoke with a new president who was pumped about seeing my dad. I still had to somehow muster the energy to preach again the next day. And now I was on the phone with one of my brothers who was hearing about the abuse for the first time. To add to the mix, I now had to coordinate a plan over the phone with my mom, while out of state, to decide how we were going to break the news to the rest of my siblings. All of this was happening while I stood on a campus full of excited people from my church while spending time with my dad's college roommate.

I called Mom as soon as I hung up with my brother. "Mom, they're finding out. We need to get ahead of this before misinformation gets out there."

She very calmly answered, "Who do you think would take the news better from me, and who do you think would take it better from you?" Her question threw me off for a second. It was a question that hadn't even crossed my mind. She was right, though. Like a death, this isn't the news anyone wants to hear over the phone. But we had no choice. It would be impossible to tell everyone in person. I was out of state, and half of my siblings live in the South. The nature of what we had to tell my siblings was so sensitive and so confusing that we couldn't afford to mince words or get the message wrong. We began to make two lists of people to call—one list for her and another for me. As soon as I hung up with her, I began calling family members.

I don't remember much more from that weekend. When the brain is in crisis, it has a way of discarding unimportant memories and storing ones that are necessary for survival. I was in total survival mode at this point. My entire world was crashing down before me, and it showed no signs of slowing down.

As expected, there were wildly different reactions. Some family members promised to kill him before his arrest. Some siblings cussed me out for not talking it over with them first and for reporting him so quickly. Some were just sad and didn't have much to say. And, strangely, I felt all of those same emotions and completely understood. Because Mom and I had the most first-hand information, it was our job to inform, listen, and diffuse. This cycle was repeated over and over again for the next several days. Inform, listen, diffuse.

None of us knew for sure when the arrest would happen, but we knew he would be arrested. On the week of his arrest, Dad called me to go out for coffee. I had no idea what he wanted to talk about, but I also knew it could be our last time together on this side of prison. It ended up being so. Unlike a few days prior, he was now calm and collected. It was strange to witness someone who knew that a very bad fate was just on the horizon, yet was able to remain so calm. Maybe it was the relief that he didn't have to hide who he was anymore. People in the community were starting to find out. Everyone in my family already knew. The public was about to find out through the news. As we sat there in the restaurant, he leaned in a little closer so that neighboring tables couldn't overhear. "By the way, just so you know what you're dealing with when I'm canned, here are the names of my victims." One by one, he casually called out the names of his victims.

My heart felt tremendous pain with each name that he calmly rattled off. It was more information than I really was prepared to know, and my heart really wasn't ready to hear individual victims' names. As he said each name, I could see her face in my head. I knew just about every single victim. Half of my heart stopped beating due to the deep, deep sorrow I felt for all that he took from every one of those precious children. The other half was burning with rage and wanted him dead. I couldn't process all the emotions. I'd experienced so much trauma over the course of less than three weeks' time, and much more was just on the horizon. As he was rattling names off, my worst fear became a living nightmare. Some of the victims were still young children. And some of those young children belonged to my church.

I went home and buried my head into my pillow and sobbed. I was screaming so loud that I went hoarse. God will have to forgive me for the string of cuss words that spilled out of my mouth. I had an un-controlled pouring out of rage and sadness. My wife got home from work, and she could see the exhaustion on my face. I wore it all over my body. My mind and soul were completely depleted. I literally had nothing left inside of me. I was nearing a mental breakdown, and Na-talie knew it. I knew I had to tell her who the victims were, yet I want-ed so badly to protect her heart, too. This wasn't her burden to bear. She didn't sign up for this when she married me. But I had nobody else to talk to. There was nobody from church I could talk to about it yet. Not these details, anyway.

I went through the list of names with my wife. I waited until the very end to name the little girls from church. When I said their names out loud, I completely broke down again, sobbing uncontrollably. It was the first time since we had been married that Natalie saw me completely break down. Natalie instinctively reached over and held me in her arms. We wept together in total silence for a long time. "Honey, if. . ." I couldn't get the words out because my mind couldn't go there. "If this was. . ." Just the thought of where my mind was going kept stopping the words from coming out, but I had to say it. "If this was *our daughter. . .*" I began to sob again at the thought. As a father, I couldn't imagine what it would feel like to find out that someone I trusted raped my little baby. After I gathered myself somewhat, I continued: "Would we want the first knock on the door to be from the police or our minister?"

She held my hand, and I felt an incredible calmness. The way that she treated me in that moment is a gift that I will never forget. She softly answered, "Listen to your heart. You know the answer." There was a long pause. "And I am going with you."

Once again, I was trying to process it all. Of course, when a child from church is abused, the news should come from the pastor. But this was far more complicated. The abuser was my own father, and I happened to be their pastor. I used to be a professional truck driver. I've logged well over a million miles in my lifetime. And the hardest mile I ever drove was from my house to another family's house to break the news to them that my own father—their former preacher—had molested their precious children.

There are very few things that rattle me. I've seen a lot over the span of my life, and it takes a lot to shake me. But seeing the look on my dear friends' faces as I told them that their babies were molested by my father is something I will never forget. I struggled to find the right words. How do you begin to tell two loving parents that their children were abused by my father in the worst possible way? Once more, my wife held my hand as I struggled to find the words to say. I didn't have much strength left, and I knew I had to face yet another Sunday at church. The church still didn't know, and now what once was a church full of familiar, happy faces also included children whose innocence was stolen by my father. The pain kept worsening as I learned more about my father's crimes.

The next day, on Friday, my phone rang once again. It was the police station, and I immediately knew. "Jimmy," Detective Beckner's voice was confident and reassuring. "We've got your father in custody without incident. It won't be in the newspaper until Monday. Now is the time to tell your church." And just like that, one more layer of pain was added. It was a sixty-second phone call that came with another hefty burden. So many of us were paying for the sins of my father. On the heels of telling my family members and the parents of my dad's victims, I now had to draft a letter to tell my entire church that their beloved preacher for 27 years—my own father—had been arrested for molesting dozens of young children. I had no more energy to think, rationalize, and inform more people. I felt so ashamed, defeated, and depleted. I was completely numb.

I'm pretty sure I threw the letter out the same day I read it in an attempt to try to forget one of those darkest days. But I still remember the gist of what I said. I told them that my dad was arrested for molesting young children. I informed them that Mom and I reported him, that we did not suspect abuse until someone disclosed it, and that the allegations were absolutely true. Shock and sadness were written all over their faces. By this time, I could barely get the words out because of the shame, embarrassment, and burden of having to say the actual words of what he had done. I saw the words on paper, but the harder

I tried to talk, only tears came out. For the first time in my life, I was completely ashamed of my dad and was utterly broken for the pain he had caused.

One of my good friends came up and stood beside me. He had no idea what I was about to announce, but he could feel my sorrow. He put his arm around me and whispered, "Do you need me to read it?" His compassion, contrasted with the evil that I'd been learning about over the past couple weeks, induced uncontrollable, audible sobbing. I told him that I had to be the one to read the letter. He patiently stood beside me for what felt like an eternity, and he kept his hand around my shoulder.

I slowly read the letter and somehow made it through. Most everyone was crying. I didn't know if it was pity for me, sadness over what my father had done, or fear that their own children may be victims. I concluded by saying, "And, as a parent myself, I know the question all of you parents have right now. I cannot disclose names publicly because we need to protect victims. There is no question that any of you cannot ask me. I only ask that you ask me directly, and verify everything with Officer Beckner. Please do not speculate with each other and add confusion to this situation. We need to work with facts and help victims and the church to heal."

Though I heard my dad give names, I had no way to ensure that he wasn't withholding other names. I hadn't had the time or energy to verify my dad's complete list with the list of victims he had confessed to with the police. But, alas, I told the church what I needed to, and it was now done.

Chapter 8

CLEANING DAD'S APARTMENT

The next day I came into the office to attempt some semblance of normalcy. At this point, anything that felt routine was welcomed. Mundane Monday would have been a vacation in paradise at this point, and to say I was *craving* boredom is an understatement. I purposely didn't pick up the newspaper. I couldn't bring myself to turn on the news, check the computer, or read the local paper. I already knew what he did. I heard it too many times. And I certainly didn't want to read about the details of his abuse in the newspaper.

Shortly after I arrived at the church office, the phone rang, and I didn't recognize the number. It was a local number, and I assumed it may be a reporter or another victim who was coming forward. "Are you Jimmy Hinton?" I could tell this was not a sympathy call. The woman sounded very agitated. I confirmed that it was me. "This is your dad's landlord. I read in the paper what he did to all those girls. You have 48 hours to get his shit out of the apartment or it goes to the landfill, and you're getting the bill. Sorry to be so blunt, but this is the only number

I could find to get a hold of the next of kin." The angry woman hung up on me as I sat in disbelief at the cruelty of the call.

That was the only phone call I received on the day my dad made the newspaper.

Everyone in our family has cell phones, so nobody's number is listed publicly. Because I'm a minister, the church's phone number is easy to find both online and in the phone book, so that's how I became the unlucky recipient of a string of calls similar to that one that would come in each day. Bill collectors were calling me wondering why my dad wasn't paying his bills. It amazed me how quickly they found out he was in jail, and I was even more surprised at how quickly they ruthlessly began the calls to collect bills. Having to play bill negotiator wasn't something I'd even thought of when I first reported the abuse.

Cleaning out his apartment was the last thing I would have thought of, and it was dead last on a list of things that I felt up to doing. But I was the one to receive the call, and I was the one who was going to receive a massive bill I couldn't afford if I didn't organize a crew. It was crystal clear that all of Dad's problems were now officially *our* problems. I called my brother Joe, and he was so kind. He assured me that he would get a pickup truck from his father-in-law and meet another brother and me at the apartment in the evening.

Nothing in the world could have prepared us for the weight of what was about to happen. My brother Joe worked very hard to get my dad that apartment after Natalie and I bought our house. Dad and Mom had been separated now for four years and were officially divorced. Good to his promise, my dad found another sibling to "mooch" off of as soon as we bought our house in 2009. He eventually wore his welcome out there, too. Dad's new apartment was supposed to represent a new phase in life for him. After four years of mooching—two living with me and another two living with my younger brother—he finally had a place he could call his own. Dad had been on his own only a few short months before he was arrested. Now we were moving every one of his earthly possessions out of his apartment for good as he got settled into his new home, a 12x12 concrete cell. We didn't know when sentencing was or how long of a prison sentence, if any, he would receive after being locked up in the county jail.

When we first arrived at the apartment, we were attempting to organize things into piles. There was a sentimental pile made up of old photographs and keepsakes from our childhoods. Then we had a pile of essentials. These were things to be stored until sentencing. The last thing we needed was for him to receive a light sentence and then beg us to buy him clothing upon his release. We made other piles of junk that consisted of things he had hoarded over the years. I was numb at this point and was just focusing on moving objects from one room to another. One of my brothers yelled from the bedroom, "What the hell!!" I ran to see what was going on. Inside the closet were several one-gallon ziplock bags, each filled with lotions, lubricants, sunscreen, band-aids, and a pair of children's underwear and a shirt.

Several of these bags were stashed throughout the apartment. Each ziplock bag contained the same contents. "Three weeks!" one of my brothers barked. "He had three weeks. He *knew* we would be the ones cleaning out his apartment, and the sick bastard left all of this for us to find." It felt like a game to us, and he was still controlling us from jail. He had been locked up for 48 hours, and it felt like he had us right where he wanted us. I pictured him smiling from jail, thinking about his sons picking up what I later found out were dubbed by him as his "boo boo bags."

He would take the "boo boo bags" with him wherever he was. On one occasion, a father asked my dad what was up with the bag he was carrying. "Oh, that's my boo boo bag!" he answered excitedly. "See?" With the man's little daughter in my dad's lap, he poured a dab of baby oil on the girl's bare leg just below her shorts. My dad rubbed it in, kissed the girl's leg, and smiled. I didn't learn this until several years after cleaning out the apartment when I was having coffee with the father of some of my dad's victims. I still maintain contact with my dad's victims and their parents.

Trying to reconcile the father I knew with what I was witnessing in the apartment was impossible. All the years of great memories of a man who taught me everything about God while staring at the boo boo bags he intentionally left behind didn't make sense. How could he preach for nearly three decades and have violated so many little children at the same time? How was he able to hide it? Obviously he wasn't nervous. He flaunted the boo boo bags in front of the parents of his victims. He could have spent ten minutes and thrown those bags into a trash can or dumpster. Instead, he left them strategically placed throughout the apartment for his sons to find. Not only did he fail to hide the evidence, but he had also showcased it to the parents. And now, in a final defiant act, he was showcasing it for us, too.

When my brothers and I worked our way down to Dad's basement, we were overwhelmed again. There were toys everywhere—brand-new toys. Stuffed animals, kids' games, and sports gear littered the entire basement. There were hundreds of dollars worth of toys that had never been used. At this point, we were so tired of dealing with his stuff that we didn't want any more reminders of how he lured his victims in. I envisioned the children's faces as my dad handed them these toys, of how he would have turned that initial joy into horror for each of those little girls. I remembered as kids the many times he surprised us and how important and joyful those times were for us. His victims would have had the same initial excitement that we did as kids. Only this time, the excitement would be replaced with horror as he sexually violated them. It was too much for my heart to think about. I can't remember who suggested it, but we unanimously agreed to donate the brand-new toys to The Salvation Army. Any toy that looked even slightly used went directly into the trash.

When we moved through the kitchen, we kept a handful of essentials. Cups, plates, and silverware were boxed up and would be stored in my attic. When we opened the refrigerator, we found multiple bottles of flavored liquors, an odd thing for a man who was a teetotaler. It didn't take us long to conclude that he was most likely drugging his victims with alcohol to make them drowsy. He kept children overnight at his apartment, so parents would never know if he'd gotten their little girls drunk the night before. A five-year-old child certainly would never be able to explain to parents that they were secretly drugged with liquor.

One of my brothers discovered several flash drives in a dresser drawer in the bedroom. Once again, nobody had to say a word. In our hearts, we all suspected they were full of sexually explicit child images. The police had already gone through his apartment, and I was told that they found a lot of sickening videos of sexual acts perpetrated on innocent children that he had produced in that apartment. The flash drives weren't hidden. We were angry that the police hadn't taken them, and now we had to make a decision that none of us wanted to make—do we turn them into the police or destroy them? It may not have been the right thing to do, but we were so emotionally exhausted that we smashed them and threw them into the trash. The police had every chance to gather what they needed, and I was already assured that they had all the evidence they needed. Frankly, none of us wanted to talk or think about it anymore.

For a brief moment, we stood still from the shock of everything we had seen in that apartment. Exodus 3:5 flashed into my mind when God said to Moses: "Do not come near; take your sandals off your feet, for the place on which you are standing is holy ground." The place where we stood was anything but holy. The juxtaposition of evil and holiness were felt beneath my feet. There are many scriptures about setting up stones as witnesses. If the walls in Dad's apartment could speak, what sheer terror would they tell us that they'd witnessed during the few short months he lived there? How many silent tears had been shed in that apartment? What were the little girls thinking who wanted so badly to escape the hell underneath the weight and size of his body? I was overwhelmed at this point with sorrow, and I could feel my face getting warm as I fought back the tears.

After several hours, we finally had everything moved out. It was unbelievable how much stuff one person was able to fit into one small apartment. We were so exhausted and just wanted so badly for the day to be over.

The last thing that remained at the apartment was his car. We didn't have time or energy to clean it out, so I offered to take it to my house to deal with it later. We just wanted it gone from the apartment. Driving it the few blocks over to my house was surreal. It was the last physical reminder that the man who raised me—my own father and best friend—was behind bars for doing the worst possible thing that could ever be done to children. The image of me as a little boy sitting in the passenger seat shifting gears came to focus in my mind. All those happy memories were now tainted. I could feel the warm tears work their way down my cheeks as I made my way home.

The plan was to park the car far back in my driveway and deal with it when I had energy. Little did I know that every day, that car would stare right back at me. Every time I backed out of the garage, pulled into the driveway, mowed the yard, or went outside for any reason, that stupid car was there to remind me of *him*. This car was another damned-if-you-do, damned-if-you-don't decision. If we sold the car, there was always the chance that he would receive a light sentence and come begging for a vehicle. If we kept the car, it would rot and be a horrible reminder as it wasted away. I didn't want it in my driveway, and I would never ask someone else to let that thing sit in their driveway, either. My wife and I decided to suck it up, clean it out, and get rid of it.

We pulled it into the garage and began, once again, the tedious task of cleaning out a hoarder's junk pile. On the front seat were multiple CD cases, each full of dozens of audio CDs. A lot of them were gospel music CDs that he'd saved up over the years. Then my jaw hit the floor when I opened the next CD case. Volumes of CDs from Christian psychologists with titles like *How to Get Your Teenage Kids to Listen* filled the case from cover to cover. There were several more cases with every single sleeve filled with discs that contained similar content. We had a large trash can, and we dumped all the CDs into the can. I couldn't believe how many volumes of CDs he had, recorded by psychologists, on how to "connect" with children. This was my first real sense of just how dedicated he was to learning the psyche of children so he could manipulate them into doing whatever he wanted. He could have used all of this information for good, but he chose to drug, molest, video record, and silence these little children instead. I envisioned him listening to gospel hymns as he drove home, proud from molesting his unsuspecting victims and getting away with it.

When we opened the trunk, we found junk filling the entire space. It was a deep trunk, and it was full to the brim. I nicknamed it "the mobile grooming station" because of the contents of the trunk. More "boo boo bags" were littered throughout the trunk. There were little girl's clothes, some with the price tags still on them. Children's swimsuits, candy, toys, tents, and sleeping bags were all buried in that huge trunk. My dad was not an avid camper by any stretch of the imagination, but his trunk had piles and piles of camping gear.

Natalie and I threw just about everything out, cleaned and sanitized the inside, and got it ready to sell. After seeing what all was inside the car, we didn't care if he got out of prison and didn't have transportation. To be honest, we would have told him to ride a bike or walk. A man that twisted didn't deserve to have a car. At least more kids would be spared if he didn't have a car that he could load full of supplies in order to produce victims. Quite honestly, I had visions of setting the car on fire. There would have been some sense of cleansing from watching the last remaining reminder burn to the ground. Instead, we sold it for a very low price—just enough to cover any costs we had in transferring the title.

There were a handful of boxes that we reluctantly kept of keepsakes—some family photo albums, old slides of his trip to Israel when he was in college, and some clothes in case he needed them. It's been nine years now, and the last of those boxes were just finally removed from our attic. I've only opened a box one time in all those years, and that was to give his slides to Harold Shank, Dad's college roommate. Harold wanted the photos of Israel, and I wanted to get rid of them.

Piece by piece, every physical memory of my father was either given away or thrown into a dumpster. It's a strange feeling to eliminate pieces of a life of someone you once loved and adored. I'm not sentimental at all, but physical possessions still have meaning. They constantly trigger memories and elicit strong emotions. When a person dies, people often hold on to possessions to help keep those memories alive. Parents who lose a child often keep their child's bedroom unchanged for years because they fear forgetting their child. Things that loved ones once touched become precious. My family had quilts made from my brother Mike's clothes after he died. When my mom wraps herself in Mike's quilt, it's a very intimate reminder that she can still hold him in her arms. Sometimes that's the only way her grieving heart can find any comfort. When we hold and hug possessions, we are clinging to memories that are near and dear to our hearts. When a loved one dies, getting rid of possessions is painful because our hearts long to cling to those precious memories.

But when the person is still alive and has gone to prison, it's a very different feeling. Sadness is still very much present. But there is a chasm that exists between making the decision to keep possessions or destroy them. Neither one brings any sense of comfort. Possessions trigger good memories, but those memories are forever poisoned. Everything changes when the person we thought we knew was living a lie for his entire life. Even if we remove all physical possessions, we can't erase memories. Often for abuse victims, memories are invasive. They are painful, and they do not go away. The cruel irony is that the more we try to forget, the more we remember.

Chapter 9

WHERE WERE YOU, GOD?

In the weeks following my dad's arrest, I found myself questioning everything I thought I knew about God. Until this point, much of what I learned about God—my love for the scriptures, how to think outside the box, and how to think for myself—was taught by my dad. That rug was yanked out from under me now. Not only was I facing an identity crisis as I looked back at my childhood, but I also faced a spiritual crisis. I was leading a broken church with broken children as a very broken preacher who didn't know what I thought about God anymore. It was a very scary place to be.

I thought about Matthew 18:6 over and over again: "Whoever causes one of these little ones who believe in me to sin, it would be better for him to have a great millstone fastened around his neck and to be drowned in the depth of the sea." By now I had heard multiple stories from my dad's victims about their struggles with God. Some family members no longer believe in God. It made perfect sense why some of my family members no longer wanted anything to do with church or God. Some of Dad's victims told me that they felt as if God hated them, or that they did something wrong as a kid to be abused the way they were by my dad. The more I listened, the angrier I got with God. I listened to very graphic details of abuse that my father had done to his victims that not even an animal would do to another. The trickery. The deceit. The false promises of safety, the lies and threats. All of it was meticulously planned, down to every last calculated detail. I was only hearing about some of the things my dad had done. God was *watching* them all happen, and he did *nothing* to stop it!

The more I thought about it, the more my heart felt sick. *Millstone.* If anyone had worked hard to earn a millstone around his neck, my dad was the one. He deserved a giant millstone. He caused so much damage. He wrecked those little girls' self-worth. He sought to massacre their souls. He stripped their innocence away in the name of God. He made those precious children think that God himself wanted them to be used as objects to bring him to orgasm. These things are vile. They're sick. *He's* sick. The oppression is severe. Everything those kids learned about God and sex was poisoned by the man who claimed to love them. He was supposed to protect them. Instead, he used them and even filmed them while he humiliated them.

My fists were clenched as I sat on my living room floor. I didn't want to open the Bible. No amount of scripture could fix the damage my dad did. I didn't need to look up Bible verses to see what it said about vile evil acts committed against children. I already knew what it said about it. But why didn't God stop my dad? Why hadn't God arrested his heart or given him a stroke? Over and over again, God watched as my dad stripped the innocence of every one of these little girls. And he did nothing to stop it. I didn't want to bow down and worship a God who was powerless to stop a grown man from molesting dozens of little innocent children.

The thoughts were becoming consuming. My body began to respond to the rage. My upper frame started shaking as if I had the chills. Anger and sorrow consumed me on behalf of the things Dad had done to children not even old enough to tie their own shoes. I was trying to yell at God, but the words wouldn't come out. I didn't know how to express all the emotions I was feeling, and part of me felt guilty for feeling so much anger toward God. But I had to release the anger on someone, and God seemed the most appropriate target. Finally the words came. "Where were you, God?" I said it out loud. It felt like a volcano should have erupted, but my voice was muffled and weak. The words barely squeaked their way out of my mouth. My face was wet, and I couldn't distinguish anymore between tears, snot, and saliva. I was a mess lying in a puddle of my own sorrow. "Where were you, huh? When *he, that animal,* was raping all those little girls you supposedly care about . . . where were you? Was it fun to watch, you coward?"

Where were you? It was the most appropriate question I could think of. And I thought it was more than fair to ask God. If he *really* cared about children, where was he? Part of me felt satisfied that I just called God himself—creator of the universe—on the carpet. Another part of me felt blasphemous for questioning the One who holds our eternal fate in his hands. But I didn't care anymore. I was tired. Tired of holding things in. Tired of pretending I was okay. Tired of preaching to a church when I desperately needed rest and time to process instead. I was tired of believing that things would get better when they kept getting worse instead. Tired of hearing Christians talk about how good God is . . . all the time. Tired of trying to give my wife the love and intimacy she deserved when I had nothing left to give. I was just plain tired and empty. And God owed me some long overdue answers.

Where were you, God? I really didn't expect an answer. If he was half the God I thought he was, it meant that while my dad was molesting his victims, he was exactly where I expected him to be—in the same room as the children. That wasn't exactly a comforting thought. I'd released weeks' worth of rage, but I didn't feel any better. I don't remember exactly when or how it happened, but I remember hearing God answer that day. To be honest, I didn't expect an answer that quickly. I just felt as if I earned the right to be angry with God over all the injustices he'd allowed. I didn't hear a voice or experience anything out of the ordinary, but somehow I got an answer that left me strangely satisfied and afraid. It was a four-word answer that forever changed the course of my life. *"Where were my people?"*

Where were my people? Of course! Though my question was appropriate, it wasn't the best question. I already knew where God was, even though I didn't like it. But all the people, me included, who are charged with being protectors of children—where were *we*? Where was *I* when my dad was molesting family members? Where was *I* when he offered to babysit children and have sleepovers? Where was *I* when these little children were humiliated? Where was *I* when he gained access to church members' kids? God is not some fairytale crime-stopper who waves a wand and keeps evil people from inflicting harm on innocent people. He tells us over and over again to deny ourselves, pick up our cross daily, and follow him. The Apostle Paul said, "And you should imitate me, just as I imitate Christ" (1 Corinthians 11:1 NLT). It takes a tremendous amount of discipline to deny ourselves so that we can keep alert, free from the distractions that fill our daily lives.

Jesus was a hardcore defender of the oppressed. I had never been introduced to this Jesus. It made sense why someone like my dad would hide a protective Jesus from his church and family. Jesus was always painted as a gentle, kind soul who gathered everyone near him, regardless of what they'd done. Of course my dad would preach this Jesus. It was part of his process for covering his tracks. He intentionally tamed Jesus by presenting him as always forgiving, always kind, always full of grace and mercy. The Jesus my dad presented never needed his people to intervene. And why would he? People who intervene stop evil people like my father. It's much safer for abusers to paint Jesus as an all-merciful savior who looks beyond everyone's sins. In painting Jesus this way, he is made in the image of the abuser, an ally and defender of abusers. This false Jesus is always ready to extend instant grace when abusers are caught. This false Jesus never gets angry, and people who question him are labeled blasphemous and wicked.

While the question God asked brought me some peace, it also created a tremendous sense of guilt and an even bigger burden. I felt guilt that I'd treated God as my security guard my whole life, as if I could passively pray and let him do all my dirty work. In no sane world does that happen. Sure, God is our shield and protector, but we are also created in his image. As image-bearers, we are charged to mirror Christ and to be protectors of the innocent ourselves. This is what Jesus did his entire life while on the earth. He constantly defended the defenseless. He valued and guarded those who couldn't protect themselves. He actively sought out the oppressed and stood as a physical barrier between the accusers and the accused.

God's question he volleyed back to me became nagging. I felt like Jonah. I wanted to run far and fast from any mission that would require me to even think about abuse, let alone to become a rescuer of children. Couldn't other people do this work? Couldn't *anyone* other than I do it? I felt the least qualified, most overburdened, and hopelessly weighed down with grief; yet my heart was always racing. I couldn't sleep at night, knowing I could be doing something. The faces of my dad's victims were all I could see when I closed my eyes. They weren't the happy faces I once knew, either. They were crying out for help in my visions. Those images haunted me night after restless night. The more I tried to forget them, the more they appeared.

To make matters worse, I began seeing images of my dad. These images weren't in my head—they were *part of me*. Sometimes I would reach out to touch Natalie just as a warm gesture. Instead of seeing my hand touch her, I would see my father's hands. I couldn't control these images. They would come and go at random times. It affected my ability to function normally. Our daughter was only fifteen months old at the time of my dad's arrest. Sometimes I would attempt to change a diaper and *his* hands would be reaching out to touch my daughter. I couldn't do it. There was no way to logically explain this to Natalie. It was difficult to put into words, and I was embarrassed that I couldn't control these intrusive thoughts. I just avoided touching Natalie when I could, and I stopped changing Eden's diapers altogether. Thankfully, those images eventually stopped, but it's now nine years later and I can still remember how clearly I saw them.

The crippling ripple effects of my dad's abuse were being felt and seen by all of us—even those of us who weren't abused by him—and it made me wonder what we all had done to deserve his punishment. The public celebrates when an abuser is put into prison. But it's the family members of that abuser who carry the heaviest sentence. Every routine is uprooted. Every thought is invaded. Every attempt at intimacy is poisoned. Every interaction with God is muddied. Everything, and I mean *everything*, is impacted by abuse. It's been almost a decade, and the ripple effects are still felt every day. They aren't the tidal waves that they were in the beginning, but the ripples are still there, and every one of those ripples has enough energy to rock us just a little bit.

Just yesterday my phone rang, which is nothing out of the ordinary. It rings and dings constantly. I happened to look at the ID, and it was coming from my dad's prison. I was in the middle of feeding my kids lunch and didn't answer. Every time I see a call from his prison, I wonder whether he's just calling to chat, whether he's trying to get information out of me about other family members, or whether it's the prison staff calling to inform me that he finally died. It's impossible to explain all these feelings, but they are always present. Not a day goes by when I don't feel some sort of weight from the damage my father created.

Grief has a cumulative effect, and sometimes grief is relentless in delivering its cruel blows. On May 22, 2015, Natalie was rocking our nine-day-old newborn son, Isaac. We had spent the day with some dear friends from church at their campground because we just needed to get out of the house. When we got home, Isaac wouldn't stop crying, and I had just lay down to try to get some sleep. Natalie called my name from the baby room. She was tapping out to get some rest. I was just getting ready to get out of bed when my phone rang. It was one of my sisters. This call concerned me because my family never calls late at night. "Jimmy! Mike's dead. I don't know what's going on, but I'm coming over to get you, and we're going to Mom's house. She's hysterical right now and needs us." She hung up and I jumped out of bed to get dressed. Mike is my oldest brother, and all I knew was that he was dead at the age of 42, leaving behind three amazing kids and a wife.

My mind began to race. Was it suicide? Did he somehow lose hope from not being able to process grief? Mike was as extroverted as they come, but he was also the macho type and never spoke about his feelings. Any time anyone else did, he'd muse, "Quit being lame!" He was always the life of the party. No matter how bad things were, when Mike walked into a room, everyone would light up and instantly feel better. One time I was at his house visiting and, to my surprise, he opened up about my dad and how angry he was. He talked for about two hours straight, and I just listened. It was the first time in my life I'd ever heard Mike open up about anything serious. He gave me a glimpse into his broken heart—a moment that I will forever hold on to.

My sister and I were the first to arrive at Mom's house. We could hear her wailing from outside the house. She was alone. All eleven of us kids were grown and out of the house. Her ex-husband and father of her children was in prison and left her with the weight of the world on her shoulders. And now her eldest son was suddenly taken from her. We walked into the house and found her lying in her bed, screaming out to God. She was asking somewhat different questions from those I had asked a few years before. "Why, God?" she yelled. "You've already taken so much from this family. Why did you have to take my boy, too? Wasn't the pain inflicted on my family enough for you? His wife and little babies needed him, and *you* took him away from us. I hate you, God!"

Grief was not new for my mom. She's an author of a book on child loss that she wrote in 1998 called *Silent Grief.* The book is about parents who lose their children and suffer in silence because of the stigma attached to talking about death. In addition to her eleven living children, Mom had suffered several miscarriages and stillbirths, but this was the first time she had lost an adult child. Half of my siblings are local, and the other half live out of state. One by one, the local siblings began showing up. Mom's bedroom was heavy with deep sorrow. It wasn't just the death of my brother that we all felt in her bedroom that night. There was an unspoken grief that we all felt. Each of us carries the grief of a father who betrayed his family and who is spending the rest of his life in prison. It's an unfair grief from the countless victims whose lives he permanently upended. And it's a confusing grief from all the unknowns and loneliness. I've felt sadness before, but there, in my mother's bedroom that night, was the most crushing kind I'd ever experienced.

Mom apologized to me. "Once again, you're the one who has to take care of family members. How much more can this family take?" I assured her that I didn't mind. I didn't go into ministry to have an easy life playing church. Being in ministry means you experience life and death—sometimes even nine days apart, and within your own family. We preachers are invited to participate in weddings and funerals. We visit families in the hospital who are holding newborn children. Then we walk down the hall and visit another who is saying goodbye to a dying family member. Ministry is a constant rollercoaster ride. And I wouldn't have it any other way.

Sadness permeated the room on that Friday night—ironically, the same day of the week that my sister disclosed the abuse to me. Once again, we found ourselves talking about how to inform the siblings who live out of state. We were trying to think of everyone who needed to know that night. It was already after 11:00 PM, but we needed to get the information out. As we were talking, an awkward silence filled the room once again. I can't explain how, but we all knew what the other was thinking. There was a long pause as all the eyes started to migrate toward me. "I'll call the prison," I said. I excused myself from the room and broke down crying. All the memories of my daddy playing with me as a kid came flooding back. I wanted *that* dad back again. We needed our father in the room that night, and instead, he was locked away forever. I didn't want to have to call my abusive father in prison, but there was no option not to.

These are just some of the ripple effects nobody ever thinks about. The man who created all of the pain we were feeling was still Mike's father.

Even though he was in prison—and deserved to be there—he also had the right to know that his son was dead. I can protest that all day long, but it doesn't make it any less true. He had every right to know, and I knew full well nobody else in the family was in a place where they could make that call. I felt physically ill thinking about making that call in the morning. My mind wandered to a million scenarios—none of them good.

What if he requested to get a release to travel to Memphis for the funeral? What if he asked to ride along with my family? What if he promised not to come but would pull a surprise visit at the funeral instead? What if he insisted on preaching at Mike's funeral or insisted on sharing all the good memories he had of Mike? Any one of these scenarios would be traumatizing to family members. It was a very big fear that we all shared. Not only was I the one calling the prison in the morning, but I would also have to be the one to tell Dad that he wasn't welcome at his own son's funeral.

When I called the prison, they wouldn't allow me to talk to my dad. I felt a strange, immediate sense of relief. They said I had to inform the prison chaplain, but he was not available until Monday morning. I was leaving for a twelve-hour drive on Sunday as soon as I was finished preaching, and I was the one doing the funeral service for my own brother. Our whole family would be leaving together, including our eleven-day-old baby. There was enough on my plate, and I wasn't interested in adding phone tag with a prison chaplain to my to-do list.

We found out later that my brother died of a massive heart attack. He was 42 years old, was in good physical shape, and had been lifting weights with my nephew the night before he died. Though my faith didn't shatter this time, plenty of questions about God came flooding back. Why Mike? Why now? Was our family cursed? Did he die of a broken heart? I may never get the answers to those questions, but I've learned that there is a great deal of humility in learning that we truly are powerless over so many circumstances in life, including when we and our loved ones die.

It's an illusion to think that we have complete power over health and safety, and that "good Christians" are immune to abuse, disease, and death. The reality is that the world is full of diseases that don't discriminate. There are natural disasters that will steer wherever they will go. And abuse will never be eradicated. Evil will always exist. Prisons will always be at capacity. It's an unattainable dream to think that we have the power or ability to wipe out abuse. As long as the devil is alive, evil people and evil forces will exist in this world.

I think of John the Baptist, and it gives me some comfort. I don't know why I've never heard a sermon about his death. Jesus was just barely into his ministry work when he found out that his cousin John was beheaded. The news of John's death was what set the stage for the feeding of the five thousand and the storm on the sea. After the disciples buried John's body, they told Jesus about his death. "Now when Jesus heard this, he withdrew from there in a boat to a desolate place by himself. But when the crowds heard it, they followed him on foot from the towns" (Matthew 14:13 ESV).

Mark says that Jesus told his disciples to go to a desolate place and rest because they didn't even have leisure to eat. They were busy. They were overworked and tired. People were so desperate for hope and healing that Jesus and his disciples couldn't get time to eat. John had just been beheaded. Even Jesus wasn't immune from the sudden death of loved ones due to oppression and disease. I know people who quit believing in God because they or loved ones experience a traumatic event. But Jesus did something incredible instead. They were exhausted from work and sorrow. Thinking they were escaping to find rest so they could grieve, the crowds instead followed them and beat them to the other side of the Sea of Galilee. The lake spanned only six miles from east to west, which gave the swift-paced travelers time to beat the boats to the other side.

I would have been livid. I would have lashed out at the crowds, telling them that they were selfish. I would have told God that he was unfair and that he didn't even let the brokenhearted have one single day to rest. But Jesus saw the crowds, and "he had compassion on them, because they were like sheep without a shepherd" (Mark 6:34). Jesus, exhausted as he was, immediately began healing the sick and teaching the crowds. They started arriving by the thousands. And in the deepest act of compassion, he noticed that they were hungry, so he miraculously produced enough food to feed the entire crowd.

"Where were my people?" is the question from God that guides me. It's what keeps me coming back to Him. It's what causes me to process my anger, grief, and bitterness so that I can keep seeing despondent people through a lens of compassion. Jesus should have been resting. He tried to rest! He was heartbroken over John's death. He and his disciples were worn out. They needed and deserved a lengthy sabbatical. They at least deserved one day to grieve. Instead, they got more work. Thousands and thousands of despondent people were all in one location. I believe Jesus was responding to the same question that I heard from God: *Where are my people?* Jesus didn't just feed people. He constantly rebuked evil and protected people who were being oppressed. Jesus defended the cause of the innocent and vulnerable. He summed up the mission of his ministry this way:

> The Spirit of the Lord is upon me,
> because he has anointed me
> to proclaim good news to the poor.
> He has sent me to proclaim liberty to the captives
> and recovering of sight to the blind,

> to set at liberty those who are oppressed,
> to proclaim the year of the Lord's favor.
> (Luke 4:18–19 ESV)

Our kids can't afford for us to sit idly by, hoping someone else will step up to the plate to protect them. Idleness hasn't worked for generations, and it's not working now. So now is the time for Christians to act. The church's record on abuse should embarrass us. When secular researchers rightly name the church as the most dangerous place for children, it ought to spark a fight inside every one of us.

Chapter 10

THE OBSESSION TO GET INSIDE DAD'S HEAD

The mind is powerful. Words have meaning, and they can be incredibly persuasive. We can convince ourselves of many things—that the world is out to get us, that we will never amount to anything, that we are dying of a disease when we're not sick at all, and that our lot in life is to just scrape by. We can also convince ourselves to excel—that we are intelligent and are fully capable of being creative, solving problems, and acquiring or creating jobs that pay us well and help change the world. In the same way that we can persuade ourselves, we can just as easily persuade certain others. With just a few words, we can convince people that they are fat or skinny, ugly or pretty, smart or dumb, fun to be around or a nuisance.

For his entire adult life, my dad used words to convince children to strip down naked and perform sex acts on him. There were other times where he would be the one performing sex acts on the children. Knowing full well he was committing felony acts, and also knowing the life-long damage he was causing these little ones, he always convinced parents of those children that everything was fine and that he was a safe, godly person for their children to be around. Parents always complied and happily sent their kids to spend time with my dad.

I use words to make a living. As a preacher and public speaker, I know how much words matter. Yet I can't find adequate words to describe how foolish I felt when I found out that my father had fleeced all of us who ever loved him. He lied, cheated, stole, and masqueraded as someone he was not in order to strip the innocence from every one of the tiny children he serially abused. And we never noticed. Never. Not once did I suspect my father of being a sexual predator of children. And that really bothered me.

How did he do it? Every time I train groups of people, inevitably someone will ask *why*? The question may come in another form, but it is always asked. "Do you think he was abused as a kid? What made him the way he is? Is there something wrong with his brain? What was his home life like?" All of those questions are ultimately asking why he did what he did—what was it that *"made"* him want to abuse children? I don't mean for this to sound cavalier, but I really am not concerned with why. Just as I think "Where was God?" is the less important question, I also believe "Why do abusers abuse?" is not nearly as important as another question. The more important question for me is, *"How did he do it?"*

We can ask *why* for our entire lives and never get a truthful answer. Or we can get one thousand different answers from one thousand different offenders. What "makes" one abuse children may not be the same motivator for another. Honest researchers say that determining causality is incredibly complex and, in the end, nobody really knows why certain people turn into abusers while others do not. I desperately wanted to know *how* he did it. How did he successfully get away with abusing multiple victims over the course of decades, time after time? How did he choose his victims? How did he successfully convince children to strip down and perform sexually on a grown man? How did he keep them silent? How did he have such persuasion over me and everyone else so that we never suspected him of abuse? How did he manipulate every one of us into believing he truly loved children? How did he abuse some of his own children in the same house I grew up in while the rest of us in the home remained oblivious?

The vast majority of information we know about abusers comes from interviewing incarcerated offenders. Researchers want to know what their thinking errors are, what the grooming process looks like, what classification of abusers they are, what their level of risk to reoffend is, and so forth. But for me, finding out how he burned so many innocent lives to the ground and got away with it was deeply personal and required a shift in my thinking. Knowing his victims so well gives me a perspective that other researchers don't have. Being his son and having a lifetime of experiences with him adds another important perspective. The man who raised me and who I'd spent my entire life thinking was my best friend and a devout God-fearing man—my own father and childhood hero—had lied to all of us and created a double life. He severely abused some of my family members who I'd give my own life to defend. He abused church members. He abused children in the community. And he did it by using every one of us as pawns to take what he wanted. It was necessary for me to figure out how he did it. More importantly, I began to research what it was about us that made us susceptible targets of deception.

While researchers are focused on the abuser behind bars, I felt the need to shift perspectives and also focus on us as adults who were not abused. What is it about *us* that makes us blind to the abuse? By asking the question *How did he do it?* I'm essentially attempting to get into the mind of my father—to see with his eyes—and learn how he selected us as prey. In essence, instead of "looking for" abusers by identifying grooming behaviors, I wanted to start "looking for" us. Because that's exactly what abusers do. They're not interested in looking for other pedophiles. They're looking for us! Their lives are spent identifying victims to abuse, but they also need to find a community who will remain blind to the abuse. They are incredibly skilled and selective hunters. They instinctively know who to draw in closer and who to keep at arm's length. My dad recently told me that he could walk into any room, and within thirty seconds, he could identify the children he could potentially abuse and, at the same time, identify the most vulnerable adults who he could manipulate into keeping blind to the abuse. Thirty seconds!

All advocates know that abusers are charismatic, charming, and quick. Abusers are highly skilled at pretending to be someone they are not. They are very good at hand-selecting their victims. They know what to say, when to say it, and what works for each individual to ensure silence. If we are looking for abusers only by trying to identify "grooming behaviors," we will remain light years behind the abusers who can walk into a room and identify their victims in a matter of seconds without saying a word. This selection process is done long before any grooming. I was desperate to know how my dad and so many like him do it. Saying that, for abusers, "it's all about power and control" tells me nothing about their techniques. Of course, it's about power and control. But at the end of the day, that tells me nothing about how they hand-selected and abused their victims and got away with it.

If we know the techniques abusers use to identify and "test" their victims (see chapter 12 to learn why I prefer the term "testing" instead of "grooming"), we are far more likely to spot abusers in real time *before* they molest a child. We can analyze their techniques and have tangible ways to identify risky behavior. I often tell my audiences that training a group of people to become professional magicians then sending them to a magic show would be the quickest way to put stage performers out of work. The stage magician would have no show if the entire audience knew the specific step-by-step techniques for each magic trick because the audience would see, in real time, most of the moves the magician was making.

Stage magicians make a living by learning, rehearsing, and perfecting deception techniques, while banking on the fact that their audience hasn't taken the time to learn advanced magic. Stage performers cannot afford to make mistakes. They rehearse so much that their acts become routine, even boring routine. When they are on stage, the magic act is second nature. Magicians are trained in knowing how people like *us* generally think, behave, and respond to various deceptions. The same is true of abusers. They are not timid. They are not nervous about getting caught. They are not "wrestling" with whether to abuse or not. Their "urges" to abuse are not taking control of them. Instead, they walk into a room, hand-select their victims, and then begin using canned techniques to get exactly what they want.

As I researched, I started thinking about what it takes to actually follow through with abusing a child. To even *think* about sexually exploiting a young child is reprehensible enough. But we're not talking about thinking here. Abusers actually follow through with their plan and produce victims over and over again. They are performers. My dad described an adrenaline rush that he got from abusing children in front of their parents and getting away with it.

Most people don't want to think about the steps abusers take because it's either too traumatizing or it's just not something that we ever would allow ourselves to think about. I think this is why so many church leaders want to write abuse off as merely "falling into sin," a "mistake," or "making a misjudgment." They sanitize the language of abuse because it makes it easier to write it off as some misunderstanding that doesn't need to be confronted. Abusing a child—and actually getting away with it—is anything but a mistake. Thinking through the mechanics of pulling off these crimes takes a tremendous amount of time and energy. It requires an immense amount of learning, rehearsing, and acting for abusers.

I've always stayed in contact with my dad since he was first jailed. As difficult as it is, I ask him a lot of questions. I don't want to know details of the actual abuse, but I do want to know specific details of how he successfully gained access to children. Once he selected his targets, I wanted to know the next step. And the next. And so forth. This process of learning is grueling. But what exhausts you and me energizes abusers. Learning to observe, analyze, and manipulate people is intoxicating for all abusers. Getting away with abuse is exhilarating for them.

To his credit, my dad has shared with me his deepest secrets and parts of how his mind works. Maybe part of him enjoys reliving the abuse and fantasizing as he talks about fooling adults and sexualizing children. There is an inherent thrill for abusers to manipulate people, always having the upper hand. Maybe another part of him truly wants to see me succeed in preventing other children from having their lives turned upside down from abuse.

Either way, over the years it has been healing for me to hear stories from people who were able to identify abusers and stop them because of the information I've shared. On several occasions, I've been notified when an abuser was identified as a child sexual abuser after I conducted a training seminar. Like my own father, all of these abusers had successfully abused for decades undetected. One youth leader reported himself to the police when leaders pressured him and he knew victims were going to start reporting him. This man was a youth leader and president of a Christian camp for four decades.

At another large church where I conducted a full-day training session, the minister told me there was a man who concerned him. He said that he didn't want to tell me who it was for fear of confirmation bias. "Tell me if you can pick him out of a crowd."

A man pulled into the parking lot where we were talking and had about a minute-long exchange with us. "That's him," I said.

My friend looked at me and said, "How do you do that?"

Identifying potential abusers quickly requires knowing something of their techniques and objectively observing people. Not knowing people personally, and also knowing how they look for and test their prey, gives me an upper hand in identifying their behaviors more objectively. Abusers begin by using a series of identifiable, benign testing techniques—the same ones this man was using on me in our seconds-long conversation.

The very next day, an older man came up to me at the conclusion of my training and asked, "What would you say if I told you that a pedophile is in this room right now?" I told him that I had a suspicion of who he was talking about. "Well, you just shook his hand." It was the same man I identified earlier in the parking lot.

When I spoke with leaders about this interaction, they revealed that the man had a long history of "questionable behaviors" with little girls, but nobody had anything tangible to identify, or so they thought, so over many years they all kept their thoughts about the man to themselves. This man was the volunteer in charge of all of the children's programs at the church. I identified multiple boundaries that he crossed in the few hours that I was there—more than enough to remove him from volunteering with children. He had been reported in the recent past to child protective services by a family member and had been removed from volunteering with children years prior at this same church I visited where he was once again placed as the lead volunteer over every child.

Getting inside of my dad's head has taught me a great deal about how keen and accurate abusers' observation skills are. They have to be. During one visit at the prison, I asked my dad how he could so quickly identify victims and whether he could spot other pedophiles as easily as he could his victims. He said that identifying victims was very easy. He could identify other pedophiles with confidence, but he admitted that it was a little more challenging outside of prison. It could be that he wasn't interested in wasting time looking for other pedophiles. That would have served no purpose in selecting his own victims. He assured me that I have the same ability that he does, but that Christians especially are programmed to not judge others. Because of this, we turn off or tone down our ability to properly and objectively analyze people who are in the same room as us. He pointed out random people in the visiting room and asked me, within a second or two, to tell me about each person. If he was being truthful, I was able to immediately and properly identify violent inmates, ones who were there on drug charges, pedophiles, etc. Here was the tail end of that conversation:

> "But you noticed some things about them that we sex offenders just naturally get because we're always watching people. That young inmate to your left?" he asked.

> "*Pedophile*," I said.

"See what I mean? You and I can go around this room and pick out every pedophile from a crowd of over 100 people. Why? Because we understand posture, we notice their eyes, how they keep glancing at the little kids in this room. It's the little subtle clues, and the clues are always there. These guys aren't staring or gawking at the kids, but our eyes can't *not* look at kids, even if it's for a second. Everyone has experienced this. Stoplights are the best place to find out who the perverts are. A group of young teenage girls crosses the street. Some guys will turn their head so fast they almost get whiplash. Other guys don't look at all. It's the same with us."

Pieces to the puzzle were finally coming together. I learned that very little research has been done by someone who actually has a personal relationship with an abuser. The key to understanding how to quickly identify abusers isn't nearly as effective from reading books *about* abusers as it is spending countless hours with one you've known your whole life. Getting inside an abuser's head and really seeing the world as he sees it comes from knowing an abuser well and asking many questions.

I'm able to tap into a lifetime of experiences from living with an abuser who I didn't know was an abuser. I have two parallel life experiences that are completely different realities. One of those realities tells me everything I know about what it's like living on the opposite side of his well-maintained façade, and the other reality gives me a peek behind the curtain, at what was going on in his mind as he selected and abused his victims. I get to see many details about what it takes to create the façade, select victims, and get away with abusing them. I view this as a once-in-a-lifetime opportunity to learn all that I can. It's the best way I know how to express to his victims that I care deeply about their souls and that their abuse will never be reduced to a shrug of the shoulder.

The best way for our family, church, and community to heal is to spend the time learning how abusers think and operate so that we can educate others and teach them how to quickly find high-risk individuals and fend them off.

Chapter 11
A PREACHER WHO SPECIALIZES IN DECEIT

Jesus' poignant reminder when he sent his disciples out into the surrounding towns was the shortest and most effective crash course on ministry and deceit that I know of: "Behold, I am sending you out as sheep in the midst of wolves, so be wise as serpents and innocent as doves. Beware of men, for they will deliver you over to courts and flog you in their synagogues, and you will be dragged before governors and kings for my sake, to bear witness before them and the Gentiles" (Matthew 10:16–18 ESV).

Many preachers spend their entire careers convincing people that the church is where people are safest. Pro tip: If people have to work so hard to convince you that a place is safe, it probably isn't. The mantra is repeated over and over: *Come and you will be safe.* They offer a false sense of security by giving the impression that unsafe people are "out there," not inside the four walls of the church. This message is convoluted and antithetical to everything Jesus preached. Jesus repeatedly warned his followers that real threats come from within the religious community. Paul, too, warned the church at Corinth that Satan masquerades as an "angel of light" (2 Corinthians 11:14).

Persecution was guaranteed by Jesus for those who followed him. Paul warned the Christians in Ephesus to put on the full armor of God "that you may be able to stand against the schemes of the devil" (Ephesians 6:11 ESV). The devil is immersed in deception, and Christians are urged to recognize it. Satan is crafty and charming. The devil schemes and meticulously carries out his plan. In the same passage, Paul sternly warned the Ephesians that this is not a battle of flesh and blood, but of powerful spiritual forces of evil. And, according to Paul, where do these spiritual battles take place? *"In the heavenly places."* It should not surprise us, then, that evil thrives among the gathering of believers. God is asking us to expect it!

It is within the confines of religious communities where the devil wages war the hardest. Yet ironically, I can't think of any other organization in which its leaders work so hard to convince members that they are keeping people safe while doing so little to actually keep them safe. Christians are routinely urged to let their guard down when they are among other believers. Both Christian advocates and secular researchers in the fields of child sexual abuse and domestic violence all agree that churches are the safest place for abusers, not their victims. Where God's people are, the devil is scheming to blind, bind, and deceive. Yet many preachers spend most of their time steering people away from Bible passages that warn us about intruders and instead focus most of their energy on grace and redemption. It's no wonder churches are one of the most desired targets for abusers. Abusers easily prey on the naïvety of religious folks, including church leaders.

The leaders aren't entirely to blame, though. I spent four years attaining a bachelor's degree in Bible and religion and another four at seminary for an eighty-four credit-hour degree. In eight years I can't remember one single conversation about abuse or deceivers who infiltrate the Lord's church. Contrast that with Jesus' charge to his disciples in Matthew 10. Only nine verses record Jesus' instructions to prepare his disciples to go out alone into the surrounding towns. In those nine verses, Jesus prepares them to be flogged in synagogues, put before governors and kings, to experience persecution that would cause them to flee to the next town, and told them they would witness family members putting other family members to death. As if that wasn't enough of a warning, he then says, "And you will be hated by all for my name's sake. But anyone who endures to the end will be saved" (Matthew 10:22). Quite literally, Jesus is teaching his disciples simply to survive the dog-eat-dog religious community.

It's fascinating to me that Jesus specifically tells his disciples to be "wise as serpents." In essence, Jesus is telling them how deception works within the religious community and how to recognize it so they could flee. His Jewish disciples knew exactly what he meant. Serpents were very closely associated with the cunning of Satan. The Greek word Jesus used for serpent, ὄφις (ophis), most likely comes from another Greek word that meant having sharpness of vision. Strong's Greek concordance defines ὄφις this way: an artful malicious person, especially Satan—serpent.[5] The serpent was used as a symbol of cunning and wisdom since creation. The serpent appears in order to deceive Eve in Genesis 3: "Now the serpent was more crafty than any other beast of the field that the Lord God had made" (Genesis 3:1 ESV).

Snakes are very smart and can "see" how to artfully sneak upon their prey, blend in, and strike at will. A snake can be charmed, but because of its cunning nature, it can bite even when the charmer thought he had calmed it (see Ecclesiastes 10:8, 11; Jeremiah 8:17; Psalm 58:4–5; Matthew 23:33; 2 Corinthians 11:3). Snakes were incredibly wise at "seeing" the intentions of the charmer and adapting. They could sway their heads in tune with the charmer, turn their ears off to the music, pretend they were compliant, and bite when it was least expected. The significance of Jesus' charge for his disciples to "be wise as serpents" should not be lost on us.

Jesus could have told his disciples to simply "be wise," or he could have quoted any of the volumes of passages from the Wisdom literature in the Old Testament. Instead, he specifically told them to be wise *as serpents*. They would have known that he was telling them to sharpen their vision, blend in, and sway their heads along, fitting in and remaining silent when they needed to. The thing about deception is that, until you learn to think like a snake, you'll constantly get bitten by them or fail to see them at all. To be clear, Jesus is not telling his followers to become like Satan. He's telling them to be *wise* like him. At the same time, the disciples were to be innocent as doves. Being wise as a serpent doesn't mean you harm others. It means you blend in to better identify the deceivers whose intentions are to harm innocents. We must have the ability to see other people through the eyes of a serpent, and we must increase the ability to quickly identify counterfeit people so we can either intervene or flee.

This passage was a riveting tipping point for my understanding of Jesus. He was no longer the passive hippie Jesus who had always been described to me. Jesus was still every bit as kind, merciful, and loving as before. But now I began to learn about Jesus who had a mission, who *has* a mission—a mission to blend in and go toe-to-toe with the devil himself for the sake of rescuing innocent people from the grip of Satan. This was a mission I was willing to join. Playing nice with deceivers and giving second chances to serial abusers who infiltrate the religious community is exactly why there is an epidemic of abuse in the church today. The statistics on abuse are staggering. The problem is getting worse, not better. Clearly what we are doing is not working, so I believe it's best to look to Jesus for the best answers. Make no mistake, Jesus was regularly training his disciples to see evil permeating from people bent on harm who, on the outside, looked like godly people but inwardly were wolves. We'll take a closer look at this concept in the chapter about theology and deception.

Upon learning that my dad abused some of his victims inside the church building, I realized how unequipped I was at first to understand how this could even happen in the first place. Again, rather than getting hung up on why God allowed this to happen, I shifted my focus on understanding how serpents operate using deception. My dad had slithered his way into every facet of innocent people's lives and had bitten time and time again, leaving a path of destruction while he escaped unscathed and undetected. Though his victims felt the poisonous venom coursing through their veins, none of us ever saw the deception that was unfolding literally right in front of our eyes.

I started asking very difficult, personal questions of my dad: How did you do it? How did you know that victims wouldn't tell on you? How did you know which kids were more vulnerable than others? How did you know their parents wouldn't catch on? Were there potential victims that you did not abuse because they were too aware? What did you say to parents to gain their trust? How did you move from "Hello" to "Let me babysit your child"? Were there times you almost got caught? How did you adapt when that happened? Was it easy or difficult to fool us? What was the end game, and how did you get it accomplished? The most important questions I asked were, "If you were me, how would I go about. . . ." Framing the questions this way put my dad into my shoes, a novice, and it allowed him to walk me through his thought process, as I was someone who literally knew nothing about how to deceive other people.

The more I asked, the more I realized that, like most people, I didn't know nearly as much as I thought I did about just how complex deception is. If you've ever seen the inside of a mechanical watch, you'll have a pretty good picture of how complex deception can be. There are dozens of gears, all sized differently, and each has its own important purpose. All the moving parts need to be perfectly sized, aligned, and synchronized for the watch to work properly. Tick. Tick. Tick. One slight miscalculation, and the watch won't keep time. The engineering is incredibly intricate, calculated, and precise. No matter how insignificant any one part might seem to us, the watchmaker knows that its removal results in catastrophic failure. Every spring, every gear, and every tooth on each gear has a purpose and must work in perfect harmony with all the other parts.

To help make sense of all that I was learning, I began watching documentaries on plane crashes. The NTSB's ability to reconstruct a plane crash still leaves me awestruck. They never begin an investigation with assumptions. Investigators can't afford to be biased or have speculative theories. Aside from alien abductions, no options are off the table for determining what brings a plane down. NTSB investigators begin with a blank slate and start the process of objectively gathering information. They interview scores of people and jot down every detail, no matter how insignificant it seems at the time. They invite experts from multiple professions and backgrounds. They consult engineers, pilots, and training manuals for that particular aircraft. They analyze weather, check sensors, evaluate computer systems, and so on. In essence, they are putting the watch back together, piece by piece, to find out which part of it failed and subsequently started the chain of events leading to the machine falling out of the sky.

In order to understand how abusers use deception, I started talking to many people—survivors of abuse, my dad, church leaders, church members, police officers, prison psychologists, therapists, detectives, district attorneys, scientists, and abuse advocates. No detail was insignificant, and I didn't begin with any assumptions about how or why victims were targeted and abused. Most everyone I talk to teaches that abusers are simply coming from a place of power—almost as if it was their position that empowered them either to become an abuser or to continue to abuse. Maybe so. Maybe not. Whatever the case, that told me nothing about *how* they were able to pull off their intricate plan to abuse. Saying, "It's all about power" does nothing to help us understand every important detail of *how*. It doesn't help us unpack the complexity of deception. And it certainly does nothing to help us to identify deceptive people.

Dr. Anna Salter is one of the leading voices in the world on child sexual predators. She says that, for the deceiver, where shame and guilt often are not factors accompanying lying, detection apprehension (the fear of getting caught) always is. Dr. Salter rightly says that when the stakes are high and the intended target of an abuser's lies is alert or suspicious, detection apprehension increases in the abuser. If detection apprehension is increased because people are very alert, abusers will be more cautious, confidence will decrease, and they will likely make more mistakes.

Dr. Salter also says, "Conversely, if they [targets of abusers] are thought to be trusting and gullible—particularly if they are thought to be religious people who look for the good in everyone—detection apprehension will decrease."[6] When the stakes are low and people are trusting and gullible, the fear of being caught decreases and the abuser's confidence is high.

In other words, the more trusting we are of people, the more abusers tend to increase deception with confidence, thereby enabling them to easily produce victims and perpetrate more brazen forms of abuse on their victims. They can literally do whatever they want, whenever they want, and their chances of being detected are typically low. However, there is a catch. Dr. Salter also says, "Ironically, it is possible for detection apprehension to get so low that liars become grandiose and careless and make mistakes that can undo them."[7] It's this irony that brings me back to Jesus' charge to be wise as serpents. Deceivers do not look like deceivers at first. If we blend in, as they do, it keeps their detection apprehension low. Abusers will be more willing to test the waters, giving us more tangible lies to detect.

In my experience, the best way to detect and catch deceivers in their lies is to keep detection apprehension extremely low at first, then increase it later. A lot of advocates wrongly teach that simply letting abusers know that churches are serious about abuse, right out of the gate, will somehow deter them or will scare them into leaving that particular church. But this is not necessarily how deception works. Abusers are incredibly skilled at lying. If we don't know how to detect deception in the first place, saying that we are serious about abuse without actually increasing the stakes just becomes an empty threat to the abuser. A better method, in my opinion, is to be wise like serpents and let potential abusers assume that we are gullible. Document behaviors. Document details of conversations. When detection apprehension is low, abusers will get more comfortable and brazen. Dr. Salter is right. They will either begin to make mistakes or will bring their deception out into public display, where alert people can actually identify their techniques and intervene. It's impossible to intervene if we don't recognize boundary violations in the first place.

Listen to how Peter describes false prophets who he identifies as sexual predators: "They count it pleasure to revel in the daytime. They are blots and blemishes, reveling in their deceptions, *while they feast with you*" (2 Peter 2:13 ESV). These false preachers Peter mentions are not people who are ashamed, timid, or nervous. They are snakes! They revel in the daytime. They blend in. They charm. And they do it while they are sitting at our tables. Normal people would never willingly invite an abuser to the table knowing that they are about to rape our children. This is why deception and pretending are necessary for the abuser. Abusers blend in exceptionally well. They have to. Nobody would ever suspect their beloved minister who sits at the dinner table to be sexually exploiting their young children. But they do. And they do it often.

Reading letters from my dad, consulting with and training churches, training police departments, speaking to groups of inmates, and reading tons of research on sexual abusers certainly have made one thing clear for me: if innocent people stand a fighting chance at being protected, we need to become equally as skilled at understanding deception as the abusers who keep robbing their souls.

It was baffling to me that I couldn't find any books on the principles of deception techniques of abusers. I searched and searched and came up empty-handed. Then I discovered a book on deception that caught my attention written by two neuroscientists, Dr. Susana Martinez-Conde and Dr. Stephen Macknik. Their book, *Sleights of Mind: What the Neuroscience of Magic Reveals about Our Everyday Deceptions*, caught my attention. I bought it and read it in one sitting. This fascinating book, which has nothing to do with abuse, also has everything to do with it. If I were to overlay the pages of this book with my dad's letters from prison, we'd have a nearly perfect DNA match. It was uncanny how everything made perfect sense. What my dad was doing to deceive all of us was explained perfectly by the science of deception.

I've written many blog posts on deception and how abusers fool us and abuse their victims right in front of us. The world got a glimpse of the pervasiveness of this when U.S. Olympic doctor Larry Nassar was sentenced in January of 2018. Nassar sexually abused nearly all of his hundreds of victims with one or both of their parents in the same room as he molested them. Everything I'd read in *Sleights of Mind* helped me understand Nassar's techniques he was using that allowed him to confidently hold casual conversations with the parents as he digitally penetrated his victims. In March of 2018, Drs. Martinez-Conde and Macknik coordinated with my local police department and me to do a presentation on deception techniques and how abusers likely use many of the same principles and techniques as magicians to keep unsuspecting parents blind to the abuse. It was fascinating to hear them describe the science that keeps our brains from seeing abuse that happens right in front of our eyes.

It may seem strange for me, a preacher, to put so much time and energy into studying deception. However, I believe it aligns with Jesus' charge to his disciples to be wise as serpents. Understanding deception is, in my opinion, the Holy Grail for recognizing abusive patterns. Without deception, abusers cannot fool us and remain hidden. Again, it's impossible to resist the devil if we don't know the first thing about how he operates. The apostle Peter is exactly right in his description of these instinctive abusers. Until we experience it firsthand, it seems completely unbelievable that the same person who we love, admire, and trust could also be capable of deceiving and betraying us on such a deep level right in front of our very eyes. But they do, and they get more and more brazen as their skills progress. Abusers live and breathe deception. Their minds never shut off. Remember the watch analogy? Abusers are the watchmakers who must think of how every gear aligns with the next gear. Tick. Tick. Tick. They think of every possible scenario and how they can switch gears out when one begins to fail. Like serpents, abusers are dynamic observers. They are always adapting, always improving, and they never stop.

This excerpt from a letter my dad sent me from prison was an exchange we had about abuse in plain sight, and how he was able to molest his victims in front of their parents. I asked him if he was ever afraid of getting caught. After a lengthy step-by-step description of how he was able to digitally penetrate his victims in front of their parents, this is what he said about getting caught:

> That alone [caressing the child's genitals in front of the parents] is enough for a pedophile to be arrested, yet almost impossible to prove as one, the parents don't really think it happened with a trusted individual, and they don't want to falsely accuse or break up a friendship or relationship. Two, the child is not aware something really bad happened and would be very unlikely to mention it to the parents and, three, if it all comes out, how would you prove any of this? *So nothing happens except the pedophile is now emboldened to explore more brazen abuses and win the acceptance/trust and secrecy of the child.* The parents are becoming convinced this perp and their child are a fun and safe match to be trusted together. Not good. Jimmy, I hope this doesn't make you overly sick to your stomach. It does me because I lived it all my adult life.

Abusers know something about *us*. In fact, they know a lot about us. They are not looking for other pedophiles when they abuse. They are looking for *us*. He knew what his victims were thinking, what their parents were thinking, and even what they *might* think, should they suspect abuse. When I consult with churches, I always warn leaders that, unless they understand how deception works, abusers will always be ten steps ahead of them and that they are no match against an abuser. If they are meeting with an abuser, I help prepare them to go toe-to-toe with them. Yet, inevitably when I follow up, many of those same leaders will tell me that there were some "misunderstandings" about the initial information they received. The good news is that abusers are predictable. The bad news is that church leaders are, too.

It's difficult for all of us who grew up in the church to overcome our lifetime of experience and theology that tells us to believe in the best in everybody. It's natural to think we should take people at their word. But this is exactly what abusers exploit. They know this about us, and until we understand deception, charm will win against logic every time. We've got to recognize when someone is a serpent, swaying his head back and forth as we try to "talk sense into him." Tick. Tick. Tick.

When we refuse to learn about deception, we will miss almost every clue that stares us directly in the eye. I've had Christians say to me, "Why would I want to learn about that garbage?" Christians assume that we can maintain a high level of naïvety and still be able to detect deception. But this is not reality. Abusers live a double life. It's a complex double life that is immersed in deception as the linchpin. Abusers are expecting most people to be naïve. They intend to prey on both people's naïvety and their overconfidence in being able to "detect" warning signs of abuse.

What abusers do not expect is for Christians to think like someone who lives a double life, while pretending to be naïve. Some of our most invaluable intelligence that the CIA collects is from undercover sources—people who blend in with terrorists and people of interest. Gathering good intel comes from multiple disciplines, but the most accurate, up-to-date information comes from people who have eyes on the source and who know how to blend in.

Until we really understand deception, my hunch is that abusers will continue to easily gain access to our children in order to sexually exploit them. It might sound like a harsh way of saying it, but we shouldn't be okay with playing patty cake with other Christians and pretending that evil doesn't exist inside the church. The church is precisely the place where we need to stay on high alert, and we'd better know what we are looking for.

Chapter 12

TESTING VERSUS GROOMING

As I begin this chapter, I reflect on an email I received this morning asking for help. A mother reported a school administrator to the police for inappropriate contact with her minor sons. Over fifty pages of text messages were retrieved between the school administrator and a minor child and given to the police. I read the entire police report. In my opinion, at a bare minimum, many boundaries were violated, and there was a lot of inappropriate behavior. Several other parents spoke with each other, expressing major concerns that they witnessed concerning this man's interactions with their children as well. The officer concluded that "nothing appears to be grooming."

I've long rejected the term "grooming" as the primary way abusers gain access to victims, though I know what researchers are attempting to describe when they lump everything together as grooming. I prefer the term "testing" to describe the primary method abusers prefer, because I think it is a more accurate term to describe and pinpoint what abusers do far more often than grooming, though they certainly do both. The difference between grooming and testing is subtle, but it's important to know the distinction. Definitions are an important part of knowing the key difference.

> Groom (verb)—*to get into readiness for a specific objective: Prepare.*[8]

> Test (verb)—*to make a preliminary test or survey (as of reaction or interest) before embarking on a course of action.*[9]

What people mean by "grooming" methods is that an abuser will prepare his victim to be abused by showering him or her with presents, compliments, bribes, flattery, and so on. Researchers say that abusers also groom communities of adults by using flattery, stringing them along, and making the community believe that they are trustworthy when they really are not. Grooming, they say, is a way to gain trust in order to abuse.

I tend to disagree because I don't believe the vast majority of abusers typically need to build or even maintain trust. He or she is typically *already* trusted by both the community and the child. Most abusers are well known by, and often even are related to, their victims. Many of them are in positions of trust already, so they don't need to waste their time convincing people that they are trustworthy. Most of the time, they are naturally trusted simply because of their position or personality.

Testing, on the other hand, is a more accurate descriptor for how abusers know who they can abuse and what methods they will use for that particular person to accomplish it. Again, think of magicians. They don't "groom" their audience into being deceived. Magicians already have the whole routine planned out, including the end game or final effect. They know what tricks they will perform beforehand, what desired effect on the audience they want to achieve, and exactly how they are going to reach that goal. They memorize the entire routine from start to finish. They have rehearsed their techniques over and over until they are able to execute them flawlessly. For the magicians who pull fans onto the stage as part of the performance, all they have to do is quickly test and identify the best subjects. This is very easy to do when they know how to test someone. Just like an abuser, a skilled magician can identify his or her subject within seconds. A few quick questions and they know exactly who they can easily fool and pull onto the stage. Just as important, they also know who *not* to bring on stage. This form of testing comes naturally because it relies on a combination of intuition and technical skill.

A quick joke, a touch on the shoulder, and asking the subject something mildly personal all are benign ways of testing a subject to find certain vulnerabilities. We *all* have vulnerabilities. An abuser's job is to quickly find them and to learn who is most susceptible to the techniques the abuser is willing to employ. Once a subject is identified, the rest is an act. It's all routine, and it's been rehearsed over and over again. Abusers may certainly do some grooming along the way, but it's not primarily what they do. They don't need to. Every touch, every smile, every conversation means something to the abuser. They are constantly observing and gathering information. I call this "information mining." Information mining is very important because, in essence, we are telling the abuser what we believe. More importantly, we tell the abuser what we *want* to believe or what we *don't want* to believe about other people. It's a necessary way for the abuser to get both information and feedback from us. Once abusers know something about what we believe in others, they just adapt to become the ideal person who, in the eyes of their subjects, can do no wrong.

When I train organizations, I do a demonstration of this. I'll ask for willing volunteers to raise their hands, so the volunteers are completely random, with one important exception: I have control over which volunteer I call on. I've had heads of child advocacy organizations who are very keen individuals, and the results are all very similar with all my volunteers. Within sixty seconds I can tell whether or not the volunteer has children, what their ages and sexes are, what their interests are, where they go to school, and what the volunteer thinks about God, grace, and second chances. I do this all without asking them a single thing about their children or home life. There's a very specific way to mine information while making it feel authentic to the volunteer. If I am easily able to get as much information as I do with volunteers, imagine what information an abuser can get out of subjects who are not volunteers and who are intentionally targeted.

We assume that abusers painstakingly groom people into liking them, and they crank up the charm to slowly win the trust of their victims and the parents over time, much like placing crabs in water and slowly turning up the temperature to boiling. Before the crabs can feel what's going on, it's too late. But this isn't always what it looks like from the perspective of the abuser. Like I said before, that's why it's important to know the steps they take to look for *us*. What exactly are abusers looking for, and more importantly, how do they find it?

Once an abuser introduces himself to a parent of a target child, all he has to do is create the reality and values that those parents *want* or expect to see in others. It's really quite simple to build a tailor-made façade after information has been mined. I learned a lot by talking with the parents of my dad's victims. The father of several siblings that my dad abused at another church gave me this chilling account:

> I hadn't been to church in years. I decided it was time to take my kids to church and reconnect with God. Your dad spotted me from across the sanctuary and beelined over to me. He was the first person to talk to me. There was an immediate connection and, looking back, he was finding out all kinds

of personal information about me and my kids and I never questioned it. "Is there a Mrs. Smith? Isn't it overwhelming being a single father? Tell me about your beautiful kids." Your dad got so much information from me so quickly and everything he said made perfect sense. I really connected with your dad. That same day, your dad suggested that he become a spiritual mentor to me, and I gladly accepted. He knew that I would accept it based on the information I'd given him about wishing I had someone in my life to help guide me. I was desperate to connect with God, and everyone told me what a great man your dad was.

This was no more than a few-minutes-long conversation. It seemed very benign to the father at the time. To him, it was a friendly conversation with another Christian father. To my dad, it was merely a simple set of tests that lasted a few minutes, and he was now in. My dad did not groom him or the kids. He tested them. Within five minutes, my dad mined so much information that he was able to adapt his conversation, in real time, and intellectually and emotionally pin this man into a tight corner without him being any the wiser. Tick, tick, tick. This is how the vast majority of child sexual predators work. It's all about technique. My dad walked into a room of two hundred or so people that day and, within literal seconds, spotted his targets without ever saying a word to them. From there, he approached the dad, tested him and the kids, and within days was sexually abusing the children.

It's one thing to hear this from the father of my dad's victims, but to hear it from my dad's perspective was even more chilling. Here's what he once told me about how he was so easily able to gain access to children:

> Your description of testing instead of grooming is spot on. I was always testing both the kids and their parents. It was

always a bonus if you could test the parents and kids together at the same time. I did all kinds of tests with the kids and parents at the same time. Putting a hand on a kid's butt was one of the most powerful and common ways to test them. It could be a piggy back ride or a reassuring pat while a kid sits beside you at church, it doesn't really matter. The goal is to touch an area that is "off limits" and see how the child and parents respond. If they've told their kid that nobody is supposed to touch you where a bathing suit goes, once I've touched their butt I've violated that. At the same time, I made it so natural that the kid isn't weirded out by it and the parent thinks it's innocent and doesn't care.

The grooming behavior the experts talk about is all a smoke-screen, and sex offenders enjoy that they are going down the wrong trail. All this stuff you see—handing out candy, buying them gifts, and all of that—I did a lot of that stuff but never once used that to groom a child to be abused. When I bought gifts for a kid or gave them candy, it was because I was just buying a gift or giving them candy. I did that for all kids, including you all—my own children. I didn't have to groom kids into being abused. All I had to do was test them and the parents. Once I knew I had them, I could do whatever I wanted-ed. I never threatened the kids or told them to keep it a secret. I could tell by testing them which ones would go right along with whatever I did to them. Now, there are definitely abusers who threaten kids not to tell, but they are either lazy or they get too scared that kids might tell so they threaten them.

He is exactly right. When I offer training, I will first ask how many people have heard of the traditional grooming tactics of child sexual abusers. For those who have, I ask them to name grooming behaviors.

We make a running list. Then I ask them to be honest and raise their hands if they do those things. Nearly every hand goes up every single time. This is telling to me, because it shows that the "smokescreen" my dad spoke about is exactly what abusers create when researchers interview them. If they can create a sense of paranoia and make everyone else look like they're the ones who have "grooming behaviors" of an abuser, they will. This helps them to blend in even better. It's a highly effective technique. When someone suggests that an alleged abuser has grooming behavior, all they have to do is point to all the other people at church who offer gifts or compliments or hugs. This is why, even after an organization is trained, abusers are still able to easily blend in and produce victim after victim.

Some people are gravely concerned to find out that abusers are doing these things in front of us and are so highly skilled at testing us. Sometimes they express frustration and ask me what the point of my training is if abusers are so incredibly good at blending in. I take a different approach. I believe it's to our advantage that abusers are foolish and arrogant enough to use testing techniques right in front of us. As long as we are willing to put the work into learning about deception and testing techniques, we actually stand a fighting chance of seeing what these criminals are doing to test their victims before they begin abusing them. If they only tested and abused children in isolation, we'd only find out about it after abuse had occurred, and any evidence would almost completely be dependent on a child disclosing his or her own abuse.

Knowing that abusers test victims and their parents publicly gives us the upper hand on knowing how they are doing it. Admittedly, it's very difficult to objectively test how effective this method of intervention is, but I can tell you from experience that I have personally identified very high-risk individuals and even have had multiple people arrested who had abused victims for decades undetected.

This is not to brag at all. It's to say that I have hope. I have hope that we can keep learning more about how abusers hunt for their prey. My goal is to teach people to very quickly identify someone who is using testing techniques and intervene *before* abuse takes place with their intended target. To be clear, I am not suggesting that we identify testing patterns and label someone as a child sexual predator. That person may not be one. We don't know if someone is an abuser unless there is evidence, and we must be careful to never make false accusations. But there are definitive patterns that look nothing like the "grooming" behaviors we are so familiar with, and we need to be aware when people are using them so we can at least stop those testing patterns.

When my oldest daughter was three years old, we visited a church. I was walking through the church foyer when an older man stopped me. He started talking to my daughter and tried to tickle her under her armpit. I pulled her away before his finger could touch her. I asked him to stop and said that neither of us liked that he was trying to tickle her. He ignored me and attempted again to tickle her. I pulled away and didn't allow him to make contact. He gave up on trying to tickle her and then said that my daughter was beautiful. He said her cheeks and eyes were very pretty and that she'd be a heartbreaker one day. He said this about a three-year-old toddler. At that point, I'd had enough. I said loud enough for people around us to hear, "Let's get you away from this creepy man who doesn't take no for an answer."

Maybe he was an abuser. Maybe he wasn't. But I wasn't going to stay near him long enough to find out. And if he was in fact testing my daughter and me, he got a good taste of what failing his own test feels like. We need to be unapologetic in our position as parents and protectors to set and keep safe boundaries for our kids. We can do this without accusing people of being child molesters when they may not be. The man who attempted to tickle my daughter was very much on my radar for the rest of the time we were there. When I identify people who are testing others at churches I visit, I make leaders aware and tell them who should be on their radar and why.

Some people might decry that as unfair. But what's more unfair is when we fail to see the techniques and motives of people like my dad and children are raped as a result. We must stop denying that average abusers are skilled and that the average person is unskilled and unequipped for detecting abuse in plain sight. Had someone been trained to see my dad beeline across the auditorium, listen in on the probing conversation, and paid attention to his constant touching of the kids, perhaps several victims never would have become victims in the first place. When my dad was touching the children's shoulders, patting their bottoms, mining information from the father, and asserting himself as a spiritual mentor, someone within earshot should have been there to say not so fast. My dad didn't do this in an empty room. There were many witnesses to this interaction that day. To be sure, some of the church members who heard the exchange jumped in to tell the father what a great, trustworthy man my father was. A lack of training for church members and a determined abuser is what created victims that day.

What I never propose is that people become paranoid. That only helps the abusers stay undetected. Nobody reading this should be paranoid that someone will start viewing them as a pedophile because they have polite conversations at church. What I hope for is that we all develop a much better awareness of patterns of *inappropriate* touching and conversations. In a nutshell, testing begins as benign touching and seemingly benign conversation, but very quickly turns inappropriate. Touching is constant. It moves from pats on the head to tickling or a touch on a bottom or breast. Watch where people's hands are at all times and ensure nobody is ever touching a minor child (or adult, for that matter) in a violating way, regardless of who the person is who has contact with a child.

Listen intently to conversations. If it seems as if someone is giving too much attention to someone, find out what, specifically, they are asking. Are they asking for personal information about a child? Do they seem superficially interested? If so, are they asserting themselves into the lives of that family as a friend or mentor? Are they inviting themselves to hang out or asking to babysit in a way that the parents are being manipulated or made to feel guilty if they say no? If so, don't be afraid to intervene and suggest that maybe it's not in the best interest of the children to go. Watch for people who are obsessed with talking about children. Specifically, they are focused on the way children dress, what their hair looks or smells like, etc. When abusers talk about these things, it is intentional, and they are meant to be testing patterns. The abuser is testing to see if anyone will say anything in opposition to what they are saying and doing.

This chapter is not meant to be a training manual for how to spot abusers, but just introduces the concept that abusers are always testing. Hopefully we can have a heightened awareness that this happens often. Children are constantly tested. We parents are, too. And knowing that abusers are capable of doing it will hopefully help us raise our awareness when other adults enter the room with us. Be attentive to other people in the room, but don't be paranoid. If we pay more attention, we will be less likely to allow people to touch all over our children and ask personal information about us that we shouldn't be so quick to reveal.

Chapter 13

WHAT I LEARNED FROM CONSULTING WITH CHURCHES

Being a church leader, an advocate, and a reporter of my father's abuse, as well as having victims in my congregation, puts me in a unique position. I know that it's possible to believe victims and to do everything in your power to protect them from their abuser at the same time. It's possible to clearly communicate to an abuser that he is not welcome to come anywhere near your church building or your church family. It's possible to cooperate with investigators and help them get a conviction so that victims can be safe. It's possible to be completely transparent with your congregation and identify the abuser by name, warning your congregation not to allow their children anywhere near the said abuser. It's possible to learn from our mistakes, to better educate ourselves, and to create better policies and practices to keep children safe. And it's possible for a congregation to heal from the aftermath of abuse. I know these things, because I lived them.

This is why I feel such a strong tension between hope and frustration within churches—hope because I know what is possible when abuse is confronted and stopped, and frustration because so few churches respond to abuse in a healthy way. Over the past nine years, the overwhelming majority of interactions I've had with church leaders regarding abuse have been negative and dismissive. Most leaders, when abuse is uncovered, want to do the bare minimum to hold the abuser accountable while keeping the abuser hidden within their churches. I'm not sure why churches want to soar with success when it comes to marketing and building fantastic structures but are okay with failing when it comes to protecting the innocent and vulnerable. It makes no sense to me. My brain literally cannot comprehend this mentality. I know that this is done to protect the *image* of the church, but what about actually protecting the *people* that make up the church?

Over and over again, victims are told to "forgive and move on," pretending as if the abuse never happened. Every survivor I've spoken with has told me that the church's response to their abuse was far worse than the actual abuse that happened at the hands of their abuser. I've heard graphic details of what abusers do to their victims. In my wildest nightmares I can't imagine anything worse than the sexual abuse a child endures. Yet, with absolute certainty, 100 percent of abuse survivors who've had a negative experience with church leaders say that the church's response was far worse than the actual sexual abuse. This should tell us church leaders how important it is to get our response right. Some of these abuse survivors are so hurt by their churches that failed them after abuse that they renounce God altogether. I find that there's a chasm that exists between church leaders and survivors. Sadly, while survivors are isolated, ridiculed, and abandoned by church leaders, they see their abusers standing with those same leaders on the other side of the chasm.

One preacher told me about his daughters being sexually abused by a family member. He said, "If I could dig up his grave, bring him back to life, set him on fire, and bury him again, I would do it." It was a graphic way to express the rightful rage he felt for what had been wrongfully taken from his precious daughters. Yet when I mentioned my unapologetic stance on not permitting known sexual predators to worship in the same space as children, the same man radically disagreed, saying that God's grace is for all. There's something inherently wrong with people's training and theology when we are made to feel guilty for keeping abusive people away from innocent people. It confuses victims of abuse to hear people say that they hate abuse only to see them lavishing unfettered love and acceptance to the very person who intentionally destroyed their innocence. What is it about worship that makes leaders feel that they have an obligation to invite known abusers in, giving them unhindered and unlimited access to more victims? Even leaders whose own children were abused will roll the welcome mat out for child predators. Can you imagine what this communicates to abuse survivors when leaders say that they are angry about the abuse but then turn around and invite abusers right back into the church?

My experience is that church leaders have a twisted view of God. Therefore, they feel that they will be judged by both God and their churches for "hindering" someone to come to worship, as if corporate worship is what makes someone's heart pure instead of the heart itself. Little do they know that abusers revel in the daytime and use worship settings as their hunting grounds to find and molest their prey. This isn't speculation—it's what abusers do!

Leaders' bad theology often doesn't even allow them to admit wolves actually exist, even though the Bible is replete with examples. The message in the Bible is always clear: Keep the wolves away from the sheep. This is what Jesus did in John chapter 10. He is the Good Shepherd who guards and protects his sheep from wolves. The Bible's description of wolves isn't merely describing what wolves do; it's defining who they *are*. Wolves do not turn into sheep. They may dress like sheep, talk like sheep, and behave like sheep. But make no mistake—they are still wolves.

It's strange to me when church leaders' theology is "grace for all," except for victims who were raped as children and have the guts to speak up about it. Many survivors have told me that *they*, not their abusers, were removed from church because they were "causing problems" by speaking up about their abuse and were crying out for help. Often abuse survivors are painted as "too bitter, too reactive, too emotional, and too jaded," simply for telling the truth about the abuse. It's no wonder that victims often don't tell anyone when they are abused. Imagine showing up to a hospital, only to have doctors and nurses gang up on you and shame you for telling them that you are bleeding out. This response would make you want to never step foot inside a hospital again.

Generally speaking, most of us tend to think that most other people are like us. We believe that people have (or at least should have) a conscience and that they hesitate to do wrong. When they do commit sins, we assume that, like us, they are racked with guilt. But psychologists have studied and documented cases of sociopathy and psychopathy, where certain individuals do not have a conscience. I believe it's how they are so easily able to do horrific things to innocent children, lie to our faces, and do it all in the name of God. I often remind people that it's the abusers, not their victims, who sleep well at night. Abusers are not losing sleep due to guilt for what they have done. If they lose sleep over anything, it's because they are thinking of new ways to produce their next victim.

When consulting with churches, I've learned that some of them are looking for quick, easy solutions to very complex problems, and that their church funds seem to be abundant for all kinds of pet projects but somehow dry up when it comes to protecting children.

One email stands out in my mind. A church elder sent me an urgent email saying that there was a dire emergency involving a member allegedly preying on a young child. Those sorts of things cannot be hashed out over email, and shouldn't ever be handled by a lone church leader. I suggested that he and the rest of the leadership team schedule a time to consult with me, and that I was available immediately. He never replied back. I can't be sure, but either the situation wasn't as dire as his frantic email implied, or he wasn't willing to spend any time or money getting professional help to walk their church through the painful process. This is not an isolated incident. It happens very often. Many churches want to sap experts for their time in emergencies involving children, unless it involves any amount of money. Maybe this is part of the reason why churches refuse to hire outside help, making the fatal mistake of handling it all internally, and often hiding the abuse and shutting down any member who raises concerns.

Abusers know when leaders are pushovers, and they exploit these opportunities to thrive when leadership is not willing to confront, report, or hold them accountable. When I do speak with church leaders, I ask for the alleged abuser's name so that I can do some searching. It's helpful to know something about the person—what they post on social media, what complaints people may have against them, if they have a criminal record, what charges they were arrested for, how many charges were waived as part of a plea deal, what news articles there are relating to any arrests, etc. It amazes me how many leaders refuse to give me a name and instead refer to the person of interest as "this brother." In calling an abuser or alleged abuser "brother" instead of by his or her name, they are communicating to me that they want to protect the abuser. They may not be doing this consciously, but the message is still clear that they see the alleged abuser as a brother and not a potential abuser.

One of the clichés I often hear is, "You don't know how much good this brother has done for the Lord's church."

My response is, "And you don't know how much evil he's done, either."

If there is any silver lining, it's that there are churches that get it right. I met with one group of elders several years ago. It was a case that's become all too common in our digital era, one involving hidden cameras throughout the church building. There were multiple victims of voyeurism, and the church member was producing child porn using Photoshop. This is becoming quite common. Abusers steal images from Facebook, from hidden cameras in church buildings, or anywhere that they can find images of their preferred targets. Then they head swap and put the faces onto bodies of naked kids of their preferred body type and trade them online for more images. This is another reason known pedophile abusers should never be allowed anywhere near a church with minor children. The group of elders had just found out, called me to consult, and asked me what to do. To their credit, they admitted that they had no idea how to handle the situation with the church. The voyeur hadn't been arrested yet and made it clear he was planning on showing up to church where his victims attended.

One elder said to me, "The biggest part of me wants to remain silent, pray that the church doesn't find out, and hope that this all goes away. What do you say about that?" I thanked him for his honesty and promised him that one way or the other the church would find out, and that a good leader will look into the faces of the victims and vow to defend and protect them. He reached across the table and shook my hand. He said, "I was hoping you wouldn't say that . . . but I'm so thankful that you did."

The leaders followed my recommendations to remove the abuser from church immediately and to issue a blunt statement to the church, explaining what the man did and why they removed him. The elders stood together before the church to show that they were unified in their effort to protect the congregation from sexual predators. The preacher who had called me in the first place called me to thank me and said that one of the elder's grandchildren came up and stood beside the elders then asked to be baptized after they had read the statement.

Children want to know that adults care. They want to know that adults will defend and protect them. Parents and grandparents of children want to be assured that church leaders aren't just blowing smoke. They want to know that there is actually a plan, and they deserve to know what that plan is.

Nobody likes to hear platitudes and distilled messages from leaders. We parents shouldn't have to cross our fingers and hope that our children don't become the next targets of an abuser because of the negligence of church leaders. Parents shouldn't have to wonder whether church leaders are knowingly hiding an abuser in the church.

I can't tell churches what to do. Personally, I think it's foolish to allow someone who was convicted of serially abusing children to even show up to a worship gathering with children. But for the churches who disagree, the very least they can do is to inform the church *and* their insurance company that they permitted a registered sex offender to attend church, along with posting the information from the public sex offender registry. They should identify and communicate who the abuser is and what tier level of sex offender they are. They should print off the docket sheet and list all the original charges. Many plea deals will waive most of the criminal charges. A docket sheet will list every charge, whether they were waived or not. And finally, leaders should coordinate all plans with parole or probation officers if the person was paroled or is on probation.

Churches shouldn't be caught off guard every time a situation arises. People come and go from church all the time. Leadership constantly changes. Personalities among leaders are different. Some leaders are naïve. Others are zealous to defend abusers. Some are passive. Some are assertive. Some are abusers themselves. Written policies are a must for these reasons. When no policy is in place, the most domineering leader will determine the direction the leadership takes regarding abuse. Sadly, the biggest apologists of abusers are almost always the most vocal, persuasive, and influential leaders. The most likely outcome I can see when a written policy isn't in place is disaster. Written policies should be clear, concise, and have a clear chain of command for who is responsible for reporting, who and what is communicated to the church, how victims are cared for, and how to pay for counseling for victims of abuse and consultations with experts if an allegation arises.

Again, it's not asking much for churches and organizations to be prepared. Parents deserve to know that leaders aren't hiding abuse or giving anonymous shelter to abusers inside the church. They deserve to know that a plan is in place to set good boundaries and to handle allegations of abuse. And they need leaders to not pretend that they know how to handle allegations if they do not. Abusers are highly skilled and use sophisticated techniques to abuse and blend in. Protecting children from these criminals cannot be done by grasping at straws, increasing our faith, or by walking around aimlessly in the dark. Planning is essential.

Chapter 14

THEOLOGY AND DECEPTION

Foundations are everything. My wife and I bought a house that is 120 years old and is built on an incredible fieldstone foundation. The house is in fantastic shape from top to bottom. The people who built it in 1900 made sure that the foundation was very solid. I've been in several very old, nice houses in our area that were built in the early 1800s and they have similar fieldstone foundations as my house.

When I lived in Arkansas, some friends and I lived in a house that is now condemned. It was built sometime around the 1950s and, unlike my current house, its foundation was not built right. It was probably a very nice-looking house when it was new, but when we lived there, the walls were not plumb at all, the floors were rotting, and it was a hazard. We hung a picture on a wall, and the wall was so crooked that there were a few inches of space between the bottom of the picture frame and the wall. We used to half-joke that one day the whole house would come crashing down on us. It eventually got so unsafe that it was boarded up and now sits condemned by the city.

After the allegations of abuse against my dad, I questioned everything about God. Very little about God or his church made sense to me, and I quickly realized that nobody ever taught me what God's foundation was. My faith, which I'd always thought was very strong, was literally crashing down around me, and I couldn't figure out why. Nothing was plumb anymore. Then it dawned on me: If we get the foundation wrong, it doesn't matter how pretty, secure, and well-built our faith may appear. When a crisis pushes against us, eventually the whole structure will begin cracking and will inevitably fall apart.

I often ask groups that I'm training what God's foundation is. This, in my opinion, is the most basic and important question we believers should be able to answer. If we don't know God's own foundation, we can't build our faith on anything that is solid enough to withstand any kind of storm. I know because this was my experience. Even Jesus said that the people who hear his words and don't do them "will be like a foolish man who built his house on the sand." A house built on sand may look nice and might appear to be solid, but the reality is that it's on a bad foundation, and one day the whole thing will come crashing down. Or, as Jesus said, "Great is the fall of it."

Most of the answers I receive to my question about God's foundation are things like love, grace, mercy, and salvation. But do we know the real answer? Do you know the answer right now without looking it up? The answer is righteousness and justice: "Righteousness and justice are the foundation of your throne; steadfast love and faithfulness go before you" (Psalm 89:14). Righteousness–the Hebrew word is צֶדֶק (*tsedeq*), which was a term used for balancing scales. It means doing what is right, fair, and honest while not tipping the scales (either showing favoritism or targeting) for anyone. Justice—the Hebrew word is מִשְׁפָּט (*mishpat*), which means judgment or the act of deciding a case. Righteousness and justice are married throughout the scriptures, from cover to cover. They cannot be divorced from each other. Remove one and the other doesn't make any sense. You can't get away from it. This *is* God's foundation.

God doesn't tip the scales for any of us. Tipping the scales creates imbalance and is dishonest. In antiquity, using unbalanced scales in the marketplace was dishonorable and would bring shame on a family if the seller was caught cheating the scales. God never says about oppressors, "Yes, what he did was evil, but you have no idea how much good this brother has done." God doesn't make excuses for any of us. God's judgments about us are rooted in His righteousness, so that he judges us fairly based on our words and actions.

Righteousness—the ability to rationally and without preference judge what is right and fair and true—is who God is. If I had shown favoritism or support for my dad when my sister reported to me, I would have been tipping the scales in his favor, and justice would have been perverted. Righteousness fails to be righteous when we put a finger on one side of the scale for anyone, regardless of who they are. Jeffery Epstein, Larry Nassar, Darrell Gilyard, and so many other sexual predators had people tipping the scales for them. They got away with abuse and produced many more victims because people skirted righteousness, intentionally turning a blind eye to the abuse, and placing friendship over truth and the protection of innocents.

God judges cases based on balanced scales. Always. This is the only way to make proper judgment, which *is* true justice. God is not the only one who is called to be just, either. Over and over again, God calls his people to exercise righteousness and justice. This isn't some abstract idea. It is *the* foundation God sits on! You want something that will endure the test of time and can weather any storm? Build it on a solid foundation.

Anything that replaces righteousness and justice is antithetical to God's foundation. Placing love as God's foundation sounds nice, but is absolutely false to think that love is the foundation. Unless steadfast love and faithfulness flow from the foundation of righteousness and justice, they will become whatever we define them to be. Look at how screwed up our definition of love is in Western society. It's become an emotional monstrosity. Whatever you "feel" makes you happy, must be love. I've witnessed parents begrudgingly bless their child's relationship with an abusive partner by saying, "As long as she's happy." Righteousness and justice would never allow a parent to send their child off to marry an abuser. Can we really expect there to be any form of justice or safety for abuse victims when leaders model a love that doesn't flow from a foundation of righteousness and justice?

False foundations are why survivors are told to forgive and move on. It's why churches keep insisting on inviting in and even hiring convicted child rapists. Literally nothing is required of the abuser while the heavy burden of forgiving and reconciling is placed on the shoulders of the abused. It makes no sense if we really understand God's foundation of righteousness and justice. Righteousness requires people to behave righteously. Justice requires those who do not to be rebuked and kept away from anyone they intend to harm.

My friends Megan and Dominique Benninger started a database in February of 2020 to track convicted and credibly accused abusers in the Baptist church. As of this writing, 498 individuals are listed on their website, BaptistAccountability.org. Of those, 374 have been convicted, 47 have been covered up by the church, and 77 individuals have credible allegations of abuse.[10] The vast majority of these individuals were (or are) either pastors or had church leaders rush to their defense and hide them away inside the church. An excerpt from a news story about a school teacher and youth minister on

BaptistAccountability.org gives us a glimpse of the kind of response by the church toward abusers that is quite typical, being replicated over and over and over again:

> When schoolteacher Daniel Acker Jr. in 1992 was accused of molesting a child, churches, teachers, schools and parents rallied to his aid.
>
> They held pancake dinners to raise money for his defense, proclaimed his innocence on marquees, demonized the fourth-grader who accused Acker Jr. of touching her breast— and voted him, in the wake of the allegations, teacher of the year.[11]

Acker Jr. had several more allegations from several other victims, but church members, rather than defending the little children, instead gave personal testimony about Acker's character to the school administrators. Acker Jr.'s dad was a commissioner in the same town. The fourth grader whose allegations were found credible by professionals who interviewed her was bullied by both classmates and teachers for "making up lies." Acker Jr. was cleared by the board of education, continuing as a school teacher and youth minister, and he also added bus driver to his résumé. He had the full support of his church and community until 2012 when more allegations came to light. Acker Jr. eventually confessed and is serving time for his many crimes against young children.

When I ask audiences how John the Baptist introduced Jesus, every time they say, "Behold the lamb of God." Doesn't that sound nice and comforting? The only problem is that this cuddly depiction isn't how it actually went down. John said *to Jesus*, when he saw him walking toward him, "Behold, the lamb of God!" To the crowd, however, John said, "You brood of vipers! Who warned you to flee from the wrath to come? Bear fruit in keeping with repentance. . . . Even now the axe is laid to the root of the trees. Every tree therefore that does not bear good fruit is cut down and thrown into the fire" (Matthew 3:7–8, 10 ESV). Why is this important? Because John's message was built on God's foundation of righteousness and justice! John's message can't be any clearer: Repent or Jesus himself will cut you down and throw you into the fire. That's a strong message, and it is so consistent with every word Jesus spoke.

Jesus wasn't coming to coddle people and tell them how all people are accepted and welcomed into the church no matter what. He didn't promise to provide cover for serial oppressors. He never invited oppressive abusers into his community of followers. His message was pretty clear: Righteousness and justice are the plumb line for peace and order. Those who refuse to repent are sifted out, cut down, and thrown into the fire . . . by Jesus himself.

Once you get God's foundation, everything Jesus does throughout his ministry begins to make so much more sense. The foundation is why he said millstones and drownings were what people deserved who unapologetically abused his little ones. It's why he flipped tables in the Temple and chased out the crooked money changers who were ripping off the poor. It's why he told the prostitute who wiped his feet with her tears and hair that he forgave her and to go in peace. And on and on. For my entire life, nobody could ever explain to me why Jesus was so harsh toward some people and so loving toward blatantly sinful others. It never made sense to me until I understood that his actions were all built on righteousness and justice.

Jesus knew how to sift the righteous from the unrighteous. He knew who the pretenders (hypocrites) were, and he never spent time teaching them privately. Instead, he blasted them for their hypocrisy and oppression and warned others to stay away from them. He called them blind guides, whitewashed tombs, hypocrites, and ravenous wolves, to name a few. Jesus knew the difference between sinful people like the prostitute who had been taken advantage of and the moneychangers who were taking advantage of innocent people. To the former, he forgave. To the latter, he drove them out of the Temple with whips.

Like many of you, religious clichés were my diet for most of my life. Turn the other cheek. Love your enemies. Walk the extra mile. All of these passages were stripped from their context, and nothing was ever placed on the foundation of righteousness and justice. Passages are constantly plucked out of thin air to form scripture bombs that do nothing but increase confirmation bias and help enable abusers. Scripture bombs, on the surface, are meant to comfort people who need a lifeline. They have the opposite effect, though. They place a great deal of anxiety on top of people already suffering because it tells the abused to walk away and be silent while the abuser is welcomed, protected, and comforted.

Horrific policies will always flow from bad theology. When people feel passionate about a certain topic, it's too easy to pull a verse or two out of context and say, "See, the Bible says so." Like the case with Daniel Acker Jr., abusers are constantly doted on by church leaders while their victims are ridiculed and cast out of the church. Why? Because the theology is wrong. Don't take my word for it. The next time church leaders love all over an abuser at the expense of their victims, simply ask them if they know what God's foundation is. Are they making decisions that are built on God's foundation of righteousness and justice, or are they having an emotional reaction to what they consider a "biblical approach" as they tip the scales in favor of the abuser?

Theology and deception go hand-in-hand. Theology is important because we have to really understand who God is, that he's a defender and protector of the innocent. God hates oppression, and he calls us to defend the cause of the oppressed. Deception is important because we need to wise up to know who Satan is and how he fools us. If our theology is off, we will never realize that God's foundation requires him to sift out the wicked oppressors in order to help spare the innocent from significant harm. His foundation requires us to avoid abusive people and shield innocent people from deceitful schemes of abusers. If we don't understand deception, we'll never be able to identify people intent on abusing and harming innocent people.

Whenever I speak, people often point to the apostle Paul and argue that even he, a persecutor and killer of Christians, received mercy. Why would I spend my career cautioning churches against inviting serial abusers in when Paul himself persecuted Christians and even became an evangelist and apostle? I think the answer is pretty simple. All of us have things about us that are immutable, that are not able to be changed, because that's who we are at our core. Our behaviors can change, but certain core personality traits and deep-seated matters of the heart are immutable.

Paul's position toward God was immutable. Prior to becoming a Christian, everything he did—wrong as it was—was done to please God. Paul was not deceptive whatsoever when he persecuted Christians. He did it openly, and everyone knew his intentions. He had a reputation for persecution, and he was proud of it. Deception was not in his heart. He believed with all his heart that, in order to please God, he should put Christians in prison and even have them killed. Paul didn't hide this fact. He didn't pretend to love Christians then secretly persecute them. Paul was who Paul was. He was honest about his disdain for Christians because he considered them blasphemers.

When he repented and became a Christian, his behavior changed, but his position toward God did not. He *still* was doing everything to obey God, and *still* did it very openly. In fact, Paul explains why he received mercy from God: "Though formerly I was a blasphemer, persecutor, and insolent opponent. But I received mercy *because I had acted ignorantly in unbelief*" (1 Timothy 1:13 ESV). Unlike abusers who meticulously plan out their techniques and are immersed in deception to get what they want, Paul acted in ignorance and unbelief. That's why he received mercy when he repented, and why he was so adamant that Christians avoid deceptive people. Deceptive people do not act in ignorance. They specialize in intentionality. They are intentional about using deception, lies, and secrecy while pretending to please God. They cannot do what they do without masquerading, lying, and being immersed in secrecy. This, too, is immutable. It's why abusers rarely change. They only get smarter at pulling the wool over people's eyes.

That's why Paul said in 2 Timothy 3:13, "Evil people and impostors will go on from bad to worse, deceiving and being deceived." Paul was not a hypocrite. Nor was he exaggerating when he said impostors go from bad to worse. This is fact. He was not being emotionally reactive about what he knew of people who masquerade. His statement was built on the truth of righteousness and justice. Paul understood deception because his theology was right.

Peter understood it, too. Out of fear, Peter denied Christ three times and was forgiven, but he didn't have any tolerance for sexual predators who preyed on vulnerable people while pretending to be Christians: "They count it pleasure to revel in the daytime. They are blots and blemishes, reveling in their deceptions, while they feast with you. They have eyes full of adultery, insatiable for sin. They entice unsteady souls. They have hearts trained in greed. Accursed children!" (2 Peter 2:13–14 ESV).

Peter didn't tell the church to work on reconciliation. He didn't tell the victims to forgive their predators. He didn't say that God's grace is for all. He didn't tell the church to be a place of healing for these prophets who were sexual predators. He didn't refer to these predators as "struggling with sex addiction." He didn't say that they, like us, can learn from their mistakes. He didn't say that God requires us to love our enemies and turn the other cheek. Why? Because of God's foundation of righteousness and justice. Peter understood how deception works. Peter knew that these people who are deceptive, irrational animals (Peter's words, not mine!) are immutable. They are not capable of change because they derive pleasure from deceiving others to get what they want. They're not capable of changing, unless they change for the worse. Peter agreed with Paul. Impostors go from bad to worse, deceiving and being deceived. In case you think I'm reading into this, here is how Peter concludes:

> For, speaking loud boasts of folly, *they entice by sensual passions of the flesh those who are barely escaping from those who live in error.* They promise them freedom, but they themselves are slaves of corruption. For whatever overcomes a person, to that he is enslaved. For if, after they have escaped the defilements of the world through the knowledge of our Lord and Savior Jesus Christ, they are again entangled in them and overcome, the last state has become worse for them than the first. For it would have been better for them never to have known the way of righteousness than after knowing it to turn back from the holy commandment delivered to them. What the true proverb says has happened to them: "The dog returns to its own vomit, and the sow, after washing herself, returns to wallow in the mire." (2 Peter 2:18–22 ESV)

I find it appalling that so many church leaders, when dealing with known sexual offenders, respond with secrecy and chaperoning. I have a collection of "covenant policies" that leaders have given me over the years. These covenants are glorified secrecy agreements. Both leaders and the sex offender vow to keep the sex offender anonymous, and the policy is all about helping to keep the church from finding out that the person is a registered sex offender. It also includes rules for leaders to secretly be assigned to chaperone the individual when they are on church property.

Wrap your head around that. Can you imagine the absurdity if the Apostle Paul was assigned a chaperone on his missionary journeys? It would have been an embarrassment to the church in Antioch to send someone out to evangelize who needed a chaperone because he couldn't be trusted. Yet this is routine practice for churches today. If someone can't be trusted to be alone for one minute without a chaperone, perhaps churches should seriously reconsider whether the person can be trusted to be there at all.

Several years ago, I sat on a panel with church leaders at one of our Christian university's annual lectureships, and we were discussing church policies for sex offenders. I listened to story after story from church leaders as they spoke about the church's "responsibility" to take in sex offenders because "God's grace is for all." They shared details about bringing registered offenders in and assigning a small handful of leaders to monitor them. Almost never do church leaders inform the church members when they have secret "covenants" with sex offenders, by the way. In fact, most leaders go out of their way to not inform the church that a registered sex offender is even attending. I often say church leaders have the benefit of knowing who the sex offenders are (they can protect their own children and grandchildren) and the power to keep everyone else in the dark.

The church leaders on the panel shared several stories of how compassionate their churches were toward sex offenders. I never once heard any of them mention their compassion toward victims or how their churches care for abuse survivors.

My jaw hit the floor when one of the leaders admitted that one sex offender was defiant and was asked to leave. Then he said, "Unfortunately, this sex offender moved to another church, and we found out later on that he produced victims there." I was waiting for the part where he admitted that they had miscalculated the determination and tenacity of abusers to commit crimes against children. I thought he would admit that their policy was naïve and express sorrow that their failure to warn another church allowed this predator unhindered access to unlimited children. I was waiting for him to acknowledge that their policy, which was shrouded in secrecy and closed-door deals, had caused more children to be raped by a known predator. I was hoping he would beg forgiveness for his responsibility in wrecking the innocence of more innocent children. Instead, he doubled down on the need for churches to "love on" the offenders and offer them community.

This is reckless theology on full display. The problem with bad theology is that it always leads to bad practices and policies. Real people get hurt as a result. It's not a matter of having a different opinion. It's a fact that known abusers who are protected then go on to rape more children because of the reckless policies of leaders. Our children cannot afford for us to have bad theology when it comes to resisting the schemes of the devil.

Do you know what our intelligence agencies and TSA do to people who pose even a mild threat of terrorism? They refuse to allow them to board our aircraft! Can you imagine if the TSA adopted Christian theology? Imagine how foolish it would be to say, "All are welcome here in the name of grace and love!" "Come on board; we'll keep your terrorism between me and you." Very few people would ever get on an airplane again if this was how TSA operated because none of us would feel safe knowing that they were welcoming terrorists to board planes. It is not unfair for TSA to refuse known or potential terrorists to board an airplane, even if the terrorist doesn't currently have a plan in place to take that particular plane down. Neither is it unfair for churches to refuse entrance to known predators who have a patterned history of raping and molesting children, even if they don't currently have a plan in place to molest a child that particular day.

Jesus, over and over again, made distinctions between sheep and wolves. The whole point is that wolves disguise themselves to blend in and look like sheep. Many of them are church leaders. I've never found a scripture that says to welcome wolves, or to try and change them back into a sheep. In fact, in Matthew 7, Jesus himself calls them "ravenous wolves" and says that we will recognize them by their fruit. It wouldn't be important for us to recognize them if we are only going to hide them away inside the church anyway. Then Jesus says what their end will be: "Every tree that does not bear good fruit is cut down and thrown into the fire. Thus you will recognize them by their fruits" (Matthew 7:19–20 ESV). Jesus is hardly telling us to embrace them and welcome them into the church. Just in case we think Jesus is overstating his case, he gives a long discourse in John 10 about being the good shepherd. The good shepherd fends off wolves. He doesn't allow them into the sheep pen. And the ones who sneak in are quickly identified and removed. Contrast this with church leaders who teach that Jesus says "all are welcome":

> The thief comes only to steal and kill and destroy. I came that they may have life and have it abundantly. I am the good shepherd. The good shepherd lays down his life for the sheep. He who is a hired hand and not a shepherd, who does not own the sheep, sees the wolf coming and leaves the sheep and flees, and the wolf snatches them and scatters them. He flees because he is a hired hand and cares nothing for the sheep. (John 10:10–13 ESV)

What does this say about all the churches that have secret agreements or covenants with abusers? What does it say for their care and concern for the sheep when convicted, serial abusers' *public* records are intentionally kept from the congregation by the leaders? It is a crime for sex offenders to not update their information while they are on the registry. The registry is there for a reason. It's meant to warn innocent people that a serial sexual abuser is living in their community. What good is this information if churches circumvent the law and hide that information from their congregants? What does it say about the leaders' level of honesty? What does it say about the offenders' level of repentance if they go to great lengths to hide their criminal record? It doesn't do anybody any good when abusers receive anonymity and protection from church leaders.

Not to mention, it increases the church's liability. When churches think it is proper to keep known predators in the church while hiding their status as a sex offender, the first thing I ask is which one of the leaders notified their insurance company to inform the agent that they are hiding a predator in the church. I'm not an insurance expert, but some people who work in the industry have told me that some churches unknowingly make themselves uninsurable if they have registered sex offenders attending but fail to notify both the congregation and the insurance company. I don't know, because our church doesn't have to worry about it. We have a written policy where we will never place ourselves, or *especially* children, in that position.

Sometimes I'll ask leaders to pretend that they aren't leaders. I'll ask them to pretend that they are lay members sitting in the pews who aren't in the know. They are simply parents who have young children, and they'd give anything to love and protect their kids. Then I'll ask the leaders if they, as imaginary lay members, would want to be informed by their leaders if the leaders knew that a known child molester was sitting in the pews beside their children. Of course they would! All of us would want to be informed, because that's the honest thing to do.

If we stand a chance at protecting our children, we need to know when a predator is in the sheep pen. Ideally, we'd keep the wolves out, but this happens so rarely that the least we can do is warn others when a wolf has entered the sheep pen. It's what righteousness and justice require. Abusers created victims through secrecy, deception, and living a double life. They are impostors. Nobody has the right to tip the scales in their favor, especially if it's giving them the upper hand and cheating innocent people out of the right to a safe life, free from intimidation and abuse.

I pray for the day when people can see this clearly. I long for the day when church leaders refuse to be secretive and protective of abusers and instead lead like Jesus did. Our children cannot afford for us to keep building on a faulty foundation. We've been doing it for way too long. Everything must be built on righteousness and justice.

Chapter 15

THERE IS HOPE

James, the brother of Jesus, said, "Resist the devil and he will flee from you" (James 4:7). That's it. Period. This is one of the few Bible verses that does not change from one English translation to another. There are no qualifiers to James' command, and there's little room for mis-interpretation. Simply resist. When Jesus was tempted by the devil in the wilderness, he resisted. That dialogue is interesting because the devil was persistent at first. He thought he had found Jesus' vulnera-bilities and certainly preyed on them. Jesus resisted him, and on the third and final time, Jesus replied, "Away from me, Satan!" (Matthew 4:10 NIV). What happened next is incredibly significant: "*Then the devil left him*, and angels came and attended him" (Matthew 4:11 NIV, emphasis mine).

People who've had any interactions with abusers know that they are persistent. They rarely give up. They make the lives of people who op-pose them a living hell. Abusers are masters of deception and ma-nipulation and will wear their victims down. Abusers are incredibly calculating and patient and will get close to people who allow them to. They strike at opportune times. They are snakes and cowards. They manipulate friendships to pit good people against their victims. They alienate their victims and destroy any decent relationship their victims may have once had.

I don't want to make it sound like resisting abusers is easy. It is not. It takes courage, boldness, and strength. Sometimes victims are not able to resist on their own and need to solicit help. This is why it's important for churches to get this right. Even Jesus himself was so worn down from resisting the devil that angels came and ministered to him. Wrap your mind around that for a moment. The devil tears down and destroys everything decent, wonderful, and pure. He only knows how to tear down and destroy; he will never build up and encourage unless it is to manipulate people so that he can bring them to their demise. Resisting is so, so difficult, but it is the only way to get the devil to flee. There should be no shame in asking other people to help resist evil people.

I live close to Shanksville, Pennsylvania, where United 93 went down on September 11, 2001. The brave passengers aboard United 93 made the difficult decision to resist evil. They knew hijackers were in the cockpit, and the passengers already knew that two other hijacked planes were intentionally flown into the Twin Towers. Todd Beamer would make the final phone call from the airplane, just moments before it crashed. After Todd asked Verizon phone supervisor Lisa Jefferson to recite the Lord's Prayer with him, she could hear him asking the passengers if they were ready. Todd's words "Let's roll!" rang out before he and a group of heroic passengers stormed the cockpit, potentially saving thousands of lives. The courageous passengers resisted evil that day, and United 93 left a hole in the ground as evidence that evil would not win.

My kids and I often visit my mom at my childhood home in Shanksville. Just before Mom's driveway, we pass Shanksville's small volunteer fire company, Station 627. On the hill right beside the station is a cluster of American flags that sits at the foot of a twisted steel cross. The steel cross was one of a few that proudly rose out of the ashes of the Twin Towers after they fell in New York City. New York City firefighters donated the iconic cross and delivered it to the Shanksville fire company on August 25, 2008. It was escorted from NYC to Shanksville by hundreds of firefighters riding motorcycles. The damaged steel cross proudly sits on top of a platform shaped like the Pentagon. This powerful image, which commemorates all four plane crashes, shows that victory is achieved and hope is restored when we resist evil.

The cross of Christ is a symbol that was meant for evil but is actually a precious gift of hope and salvation. Evil and death are swallowed up at the cross. George Bennard's classic hymn, *The Old Rugged Cross*, captures the emotion of the hope of the cross vividly:

> And I will cling to the old rugged cross
> And exchange it some day for a crown.[12]

Ironically, for the last eleven years I've stood in the exact spot my father stood for twenty-seven years when he preached. It was just a few feet away from this same stage where I used to watch my dad and dream of preaching one day. It's impossible to put into words how many emotions still wash over me every Sunday when I stand in that spot. It's an eerie feeling, and there's a lot I have to overcome each time I teach or preach. Every single Sunday is difficult, even nine years after Mom and I reported Dad. I've entertained the idea of leaving my congregation hundreds of times. But leaving would feel like *me* fleeing, not the devil.

Instead, I choose to resist. My heels are dug in. Standing in the same place that my dad did shows my congregation that I refuse to shrink back from evil. I will resist evil and turn evil into good. It's not easy.

Honestly, it's exhausting and has cost my family dearly. But I refuse to let evil win.

Resisting evil is not a macho thing to do. I don't beat my chest and bark at the devil. I don't have any illusion that I can pray the devil into submission. It doesn't work that way. I don't have a large group of people surrounding me cheering me on. There are many days where I get lost in the story of Jesus in the wilderness. He was alone for forty days and nights. When he was most exhausted, it was angels, not his friends, who came to minister to him. This is not to say that I don't have good friends. I do. But there are moments where resisting evil is something that is so deeply personal and lonely that very few people will understand. Few people will stand beside us through it all. But God will give the strength. I will never shrink back from resisting the devil. It is worth every ounce of energy it takes.

Resisting means that we must take a stand for innocent and vulnerable people. It means that we must choose righteousness and justice over comfort, no matter the cost. Our small congregation was thriving a year after I reported my dad. New people were showing up regularly, were being baptized, and were staying. Members were involved with the church more than I had ever witnessed in my lifetime. Friends surrounded my family and encouraged us. Then over time, people started leaving the church. Close friends left, and we experienced many internal struggles within the church. Relationships within the church were strained, and my wife and I felt abandoned and defeated. I felt too weak, too alone, and too depleted to continue. Images of my dad looking at me from the pews kept flashing in my mind. He wasn't physically there, but his face kept haunting me. What once was a childhood dream now felt like a hellish nightmare.

I had been offered a few preaching jobs out of state a few years ago, and we even visited one of the churches. My wife and I were so broken and ready to run away to somewhere new. We were suffering in silence and wanted to get away from all the painful reminders of all the good my dad had stripped away from that place. I wasn't sure if I even wanted to be preaching at all anymore. Morale was at an all-time low, and word had gotten back to me that several people left the church because I spoke too much about abuse and oppression. That was the icing on the cake for me. The very people who once surrounded my family when I read my letter about my dad being arrested were leaving the church and essentially telling me to shut up.

What hurt the most was that I quietly served others and didn't disclose much of my advocacy work to the church. Rare is it that my congregation ever hears about the abuse advocacy work I do. I have fielded thousands of emails over the years from people begging for help. Advocacy has been my second full-time work, and I've trained and spoken to thousands of people since the incarceration of my dad. It's grueling, emotionally exhausting work. But I don't do it to be energized or rewarded. I don't do it to get applause from my church. The vast majority of the work I do in advocacy is never known by my congregation. I don't do any advocacy work to please or impress any of them. I do it to resist the devil. I do it to protect the innocent and vulnerable and will always fight injustices as long as there is breath in my body.

At one point, our congregation had dwindled from about 120 down to 30 or 40 people. I was working on a resignation letter a few years back when my wife said, "Jimmy, look at who stayed. Look at their faces. These people are our family, and they are here because they *want* to be here. They're incredible people who have stuck by each other through the entire storm. We can't leave them. We just can't." She was exactly right. The remnant who stayed all had one thing in common: We all had experienced painful trauma at some point in our lives. The identity of the church had been transformed before our very eyes, and it was a beautiful thing. Within our small group, we have a very high percentage of poverty, life-threatening illnesses, and abuse trauma. These are my friends. They are my family. They identify with Natalie and me because they are living with trauma themselves. It's a beautiful group of Christ-followers that I wouldn't exchange for the entire world.

In addition to our small church that meets in person, we decided to start live streaming services to specifically provide a means for the spiritual outcasts to worship and find community once again. Too many abuse survivors are cast out of the church because they are deemed "too bitter," "too unforgiving," "too emotional," and on the list goes. These "outcasts" are beautiful souls who, in addition to being abused, lost their church community and are shunned by the very people who should have reached out with a helping hand. Many abuse survivors cannot physically step inside a church building because of the level of trauma they've experienced. Instead of receiving understanding, most of them receive insults. They're told they don't really love the church, or that they are too lazy or bitter to return. I don't look at it that way. Survivors have been badly wounded, both by their abusers and by their church. My congregation doesn't look down on them. We welcome them! Where other churches are welcoming predators and shunning victims, we are welcoming victims and shunning predators.

The amount of messages I receive from abuse survivors who watch our online service is humbling. We started live online services about a year ago. I still receive messages almost weekly from people who were so hurt by the church but are now trusting enough to join us online. Some consider us family, and we also consider them as dear friends and family. There is nothing flashy about our church service. We are a small group of people who have weathered many, many storms together. And we make it a point to acknowledge people joining online with us who have been shunned by their churches. We are not calling them to come inside the church building. For many, that is just too triggering. We are simply loving them, protecting them, and giving them the honor they deserve.

Jesus himself had a very important mission. It was not to grow church brands and see how many people he could pack into a synagogue. He entered a spiritual war zone and, in just three short years, literally changed the world forever. Most of his work was walking the streets and preaching in open fields, not inside synagogues. Why on earth did he do it that way instead of growing large churches? Listen: "The Spirit of the Lord is upon me, because he has anointed me to proclaim good news to the poor. He has sent me to proclaim liberty to the captives and recovering sight to the blind, to set at liberty those who are oppressed, to proclaim the year of the Lord's favor" (Luke 4:18–19 ESV). Righteousness and justice. Resisting the devil by protecting the innocent and vulnerable while fighting poverty and oppression. Jesus' mission is our mission. Jesus' mission is the reason that multitudes sought him out for help. And, ironically, his mission is the reason many religious leaders wanted to harm and kill him.

The church is commanded to continue this mission. Jesus didn't have a massive budget, a modern facility, or an abundance of people and resources to meet the needs of the poor and oppressed. In fact, he was dirt poor himself. He was born into a poor family, and he was supported by a group of Galilean women throughout his three-year ministry. He devoted none of his time to building huge church structures, organizing worship teams, putting together welcome packets, or creating church programs that would attract the lost. In many respects, Jesus and his disciples did more with nothing than we do today with everything. Jesus' brother James also said, "Religion that is pure and undefiled before God, the Father, is this: to visit orphans and widows in their affliction, and to keep oneself unstained from the world" (James 1:27). Again, the mission is simple and unchanging—find those who are cast aside, oppressed, or suffering, and help them in their affliction.

Like Centralia, Pennsylvania, the church's fire rages on just beneath the surface. There is no sugar-coating the issue of abuse. It's been burning and spreading for far too long because people are failing to offer resistance. Instead, they keep turning a blind eye to abuse, remaining silent, and inviting wolves in to devour the flock. But there is hope. We can begin—we *must* begin—resisting now. It will be hard. It will require sacrifice. But when we resist evil, the devil *will* flee. What we do at my congregation can be done anywhere. There is no magic formula. We simply need to have the courage to oppose evil and nurture those who have lost so much. Like the twisted cross that is proudly displayed in Shanksville, I pray our tattered lives can be a testament on a shining hill that says, "Evil will not prevail." When other churches join this effort to resist, there is hope. Hope for the wounded. Hope for the innocent. And hope that more churches will be safe havens for people who actually need protection.

Endnotes

1 https://en.wikipedia.org/wiki/Centralia_mine_fire

2 https://www.cdc.gov/violenceprevention/childabuseandneglect/EconomicCost.html

3 https://archive.triblive.com/news/minister-sentenced-for-fraud-scheme/

4 "Can a Dying Church Find Life? Six Radical Steps to 'Yes,'" in *Church Answers*, a blog by Thom Rainer, https://thomrainer.com/2013/04/can-a-dying-church-find-life-six-radical-steps-to-yes/

5 https://biblehub.com/greek/3789.htm

6 Anna C. Salter, Ph.D. *Predators: Pedophiles, Rapists, & Other Sex Offenders.* (New York: Basic Books, 2003), 199–200.

7 Ibid. p. 200.

8 https://www.merriam-webster.com/dictionary/groom

9 https://www.merriam-webster.com/dictionary/test

10 https://baptistaccountability.org/

11 https://www.al.com/spotnews/2012/03/shelby_county_grand_jury_hears.html

12 https://www.hymnal.net/en/hymn/h/618

CPSIA information can be obtained
at www.ICGtesting.com
Printed in the USA
LVHW030930210221
679521LV00004B/459